DESIGNING HEALTHY BOUNDARIES

A Guide to Embracing *Self-Love*,
Building *Better Boundaries*,
and Protecting Your *Peace*

SHAINNA ALI, PHD

Author of *The Self-Love Workbook*

Published by:
Ulysses Press
PO Box 3440
Berkeley, CA 94703
www.ulyssespress.com

ISBN: 978-1-64604-408-5
Library of Congress Control Number: 2022936245

Printed in the United States by Versa Press
10 9 8 7 6 5 4 3 2 1

Acquisitions editor: Casie Vogel
Managing editor: Claire Chun
Project editor: Renee Rutledge
Editor: Kirsten Janene-Nelson
Front cover and interior design: Winnie Liu
Cover art: © Thaiview/shutterstock.com
Interior art: © shutterstock.com—chapter title graphic © winterbee, pencil icon © RaulAlmu,
    folder icon © Idrisalfath

CONTENTS

CHAPTER 6: BOUNDARY DOMAINS: WHAT DO YOU BELIEVE?

CHAPTER 7: BOUNDARY DOMAINS: HOW DO YOU FIND BALANCE?

CHAPTER 8: BOUNDARY DOMAINS: WHERE DO YOU HAVE THE OPPORTUNITY TO GROW?

CHAPTER 9: BOUNDARY LEVELS

WELCOME

Before you turn one more page, please take a brief moment to pause. Allow yourself one deep, glorious inhale, and one equally impactful exhale. Here you are. You have made it to an important milestone in your journey. Chances are you have felt called to this book due to having trouble with boundaries—or trouble *without* boundaries. Maybe you've previously invested in this worthwhile process but have met difficulties along the way. Perhaps you're beginning to realize that boundaries, while often challenging, are crucial for your well-being.

On top of this, you may be coming to grips with the reality that, while you're convinced you will benefit from healthy boundaries, you may not feel confident in your ability to create and maintain them. So here you are. Despite all the obstacles you've encountered before finding your way to this book, you haven't given up. While you have endured hardship, deep down you know you are worthy of peace and are capable of creating healthy boundaries. You're absolutely right. Below you'll find the first of many prompts in the book where you can take a moment to reflect and record your experience.

REFLECTION

What has brought you to this place in your journey? How do you see boundaries? What emotions arise as you reflect?

_____

_____

_____

_____

_____

_____

_____

_____

_____

HOW DO YOU VIEW BOUNDARIES?

To answer this question, consider what your experience of boundaries is right now.

_____

_____

✎ VISUALIZATION: IMAGERY

When you close your eyes and consider a boundary, what image comes to mind? You can use the space below to sketch an image. After drafting your illustration, reflect on the questions below.

What does this image say about how you may perceive boundaries? For example, does the visual depict one boundary or several? Does it appear strong or fragile? Rigid or flexible?

_____

_____

_____

_____

_____

_____

· · · · · · ·

If we lack healthy boundaries, we're more likely to endure uncomfortable emotions, unhealthy thoughts, and negative consequences. When we face boundary challenges time and time again, we tend to develop an unpleasant association with boundaries, not necessarily because boundaries are terrible, but because our previous experiences, as informed by poor boundaries, have been undesirable.

To explore this association, let's take a closer look into how faulty boundaries can cause you to experience uncomfortable emotions, unhealthy thoughts, and negative consequences.

If you're not aware of where you need boundaries, life can be very confusing. You may become indecisive and find yourself on the fence more often than not, wondering what to do next. Should you continue with your career path? Are you with the person you want to spend the rest of your life with? Even seemingly safe choices can leave you fraught with stress. When the big questions arise, I personally become consumed with the fear of making the wrong decision. This may cause me to procrastinate or avoid the process altogether. If I do select a choice, I may still have bouts of uncertainty and a sense of regret shortly thereafter. I inevitability question my judgment. Did I do the right thing? Sometimes this daunting question bleeds into the future and I become intimidated by what will happen next. Will I do the right thing next time? As this crippling unsureness permeates through my life, I may even find myself questioning: What am I doing? When am I going to break this cycle? Who am I?

REFLECTION

Do any of the questions above resonate? In what way?

_____

_____

_____

_____

_____

BREAKING THE CYCLE OF UNCERTAINTY

Experiencing a variety of boundary challenges can make us feel *helpless*, which may lead us to be critical of ourselves. When this goes too far and we feel *hopeless,* we may also believe that something must be wrong with us, and this may cause us to feel *inadequate*. In this phase of defeat, we may find ourselves depleted and questioning our self-worth. When we're burned out, we may recede from things that drain us and struggle to find the energy to engage with the activities and people who once brought us joy.

Living with an underlying uncertainty within ourselves can also make us feel insecure in our interpersonal relationships. So then, not only are we in a cycle of overthinking our own thoughts, feelings, and behaviors—we may also fall into the cyclone of jumping to conclusions as we nervously interpret others' thoughts, feelings, and behaviors. And though it's bad enough when we fall into this pattern in unfamiliar territory, such as with strangers, it can feel even worse when this confusion seeps into our most loving, secure relationships.

Sometimes this uncertainty exists only in our inner worlds, and we're able to keep our worries to ourselves. However, especially over time, uncertainty can often end up being displayed in our behaviors and choices—even our aura. Even in the healthiest of relationships, a strong uncertainty in one individual can start to evoke a similar hesitance in another. Unfortunately, if we don't know ourselves, we can't expect others to genuinely know us either.

For example, we all prefer to receive love in a particular way. But even the most loving and well-intentioned of our loved ones can't be expected to predict our preferences. Knowing our own needs helps us to communicate those with others. Lack of clarity can be interpreted as nonchalance at the very least. Over time this lack of definition can grow, and others may perceive us to be careless or even disrespectful of the bond we share with them. This miscommunication can become disheartening and can lead them to withdraw.

Whether or not we're able to connect this to our original confusion, we may end up feeling overlooked, disrespected, or unworthy. (For example, if your neighbors have been throwing loud parties every night for weeks and you haven't shared how they are affecting your rest or asked them to quiet down, you may feel unseen, unacknowledged, and invalidated as a reflection of your inability to recognize and respect your own self.) Without recognizing our potential responsibility in the matter, we may grow defensive and be at risk for wrongly blaming others.

If we don't believe it's possible to shift this pattern, we may feel ashamed, guilty, and powerless. (With the neighbors in the example above, you may become less likely to flash a friendly smile, wave hello, or you may start to avoid your neighbors altogether.) We may try to cope by being brave and honest. We may have courageous conversations and seek feedback. In our desperation to lessen the hurt, we may also turn to maladaptive methods (e.g., escapism, substances). As this progresses over time, we may find ourselves disconnecting more and more from our own feelings, experiences, and connections. When this numbness sets in, we can become a danger to ourselves and to others.

WHAT YOU CAN EXPECT FROM THIS WORKBOOK

The purpose of this workbook is to help you design healthy boundaries. Speaking of which, congratulations to you! Whatever struggle you have had with boundaries in the past, just by committing to reading this book, you're already well on your way to creating stronger bonds and boundaries. As you proceed you'll find better footing, which doesn't mean you won't feel hesitant, or even become overwhelmed from time to time. This meaningful work is difficult, and even with guidance it takes a lot of courage and energy to persist. No matter how well equipped you are, challenges are to be expected as you press on. When you move toward accepting the reality of those challenges, you can benefit from thinking about how you can be loving to yourself in this journey.

One foundational way to start to infuse self-love into this journey is to intentionally set space to prioritize and invest in boundaries. Sometimes this begins with a literal place. Where can you comfortably explore your boundaries? What environment allows you to let your guard down and sit with your truth, no matter how uncomfortable it may become? It can be helpful to ponder the opposite as well. What places would you benefit from steering clear from while you're reflecting on your boundaries? Being mindful of these settings can assist you in both encouraging your efforts and avoiding hurdles in your boundary journey.

Beyond physical space, it can be helpful to set aside time for reflection. Without carving time into your schedule, your best intentions of designing healthy boundaries cannot rise to fruition. It takes time to heighten our awareness, allow broader perspectives, assess past experiences, learn about parameters, and contemplate what serves us best. Even when our hearts are in the right place, healthy boundaries cannot be designed overnight. Knowing this, it is important to create a habit of setting time aside to address your boundaries. Pace yourself in the process, finding space for grace when you need to pause, reevaluate, disconnect, and recuperate. And don't forget to offer yourself meaningful encouragement throughout the journey.

In this book you'll find three kinds of opportunities to help you deepen your understanding of boundaries and widen your scope of what designing healthy boundaries may look like in your world. Some offer the chance to reflect on your experience as it relates to what you've just read. Others encourage a deeper engagement in more of an activity format. The third will integrate what you're learning to someone else's experience. Keep in mind that your responses to the prompts and activities may change, and the true health of this boundary-design process comes with continuing it in the long run. I hope you will create a habit of revisiting this workbook over time. Note, too, that though there is space for you to explore the process here in these pages, you may find it helpful to record your observations in a separate notebook or on your device. Dating your work can help to improve your reflection over time.

The flexible framework presented in this book is intended to incorporate your unique identity. Please do not interpret any suggestions as "musts" or "have to's." While the methods provided are designed to suit common boundary hurdles, each situation, and person, is unique. Hence, you will not find specific suggestions to convey to others in the process. Instead, you are encouraged to explore the tenets of healthy boundary design as you tailor what words you find appropriate in each unique scenario. Although this book serves as a guide, the expert in you is you. Stay attuned to your truest self, as it will serve as a compass on the path ahead.

While this book's methodology of designing healthier boundaries is grounded in self-love, that doesn't mean it must be used alone. Healing, especially when going against what we were told is the norm, can feel like a lonely path, but it does not need to be. You can reflect on your personal perspective with the help of others, such as in a support group, in a partnership, or with the aid of a therapist. Folks who are on parallel paths can provide accountability to each other. You can even strengthen relationships with loved ones by using this guide in tandem with them. If you find yourself stuck in the process, seeking professional help can assist you in bridging the gap.

Note that incorporating self-love into your boundary-design process will benefit more than just you. Self-love gives us the opportunity to foster healthy interpersonal relationships as well. Hence, boundaries grounded in self-love can better help us love ourselves and others. Boundaries don't always need to function as a defense system; they can be a catalyst for understanding, respect, and connection. Everyone you interact with can benefit from your having boundaries whether you love them or not. When we zoom out to a consider a wider perspective, you'll see the benefit from maintaining general boundaries with strangers. Infusing love into the boundary-design process doesn't mean that you must love someone to have boundaries with them, or that love is the end goal with boundary setting. What it means is that, even in the most challenging dynamics—such as those encapsulated in danger and violence—you can benefit from returning to self-love to find your footing, be reminded of your worth, and heal your wounds.

THE PATH FORWARD

Reflection is essential throughout the process of tailoring healthy boundaries. In chapters 1 through 4 you'll have a chance to reflect on the process from a wide lens. Then, in chapters 5 through 9, you will explore the scope of boundaries and uncover a variety of areas in which you may benefit from forming boundaries. Finally, in chapters 10 through 12 you'll apply the framework of healthy boundary design, which is a three-phase process: creation, assertion, and healing.

I'm so glad to take this journey with you!

CHAPTER 1

THE FOUNDATION OF HEALTHY BOUNDARY DESIGN

WHAT ARE BOUNDARIES?

REFLECTION

What is your definition of a boundary?

_____

_____

_____

_____

_____

Boundaries are parameters that promote safety. These essential borders help to remind us of who we are and what is most meaningful to us. They foster stability, respect, and harmony in our inner world and the world in which we live. In their optimal form, boundaries protect us as well as the people around us. On a map, clear lines distinguish one entity from another. These topographical demarcations are vital for the traveler. They assist in finding your present location, mapping your adventure and navigating through the journey. Our personal boundaries help us to acknowledge what we require in finding alignment and pursuing happiness. Our interpersonal boundaries offer a social code that we value upholding—as we both respect ourselves and demonstrate how we wish to be respected, too.

While boundaries are pragmatic, they are often unclear. This lack of clarity commonly begins with what they are, naturally progresses into why they are important, and falls into the often quite daunting pit of how to effectively design them. Without this understanding, we cannot create a solid foundation. Even if we attempt to move forward with building boundaries, our efforts are futile—as these walls are destined to falter from unsteady ground. Even in the slim chance we are able to erect a resilient structure despite the underlying terrain, after facing the elements of outside pressure it would likely erode over time. As a result, without clarity in the process of boundary creation and management, we are vulnerable to danger.

REFLECTION

Throughout the course of your life you've encountered many examples of boundaries; some boundaries are your own, while others you've observed in relation to others. What examples come to mind when you consider the parameters you've observed others holding (e.g., family, friends, community)? What have your own experiences with boundaries looked like? What triumphs have you had with boundaries? What difficulties have you had with boundaries? What emotions arise when you reflect on these memories?

_____

_____

_____

_____

_____

_____

_____

✎ BOUNDARY HUNTING

Choose one day this week to go boundary hunting. As you progress through your day, use your journal or notebook to keep a running list of all the boundaries you see. Perhaps you recognize that your morning alarm is both a boundary with yourself and an interpersonal boundary with your workplace—in that it's important to you to arrive on time. Once at work, you may notice how a few colleagues saunter in late to your morning meeting. At the end of the day, reflect on what these boundaries are, what purposes they serve, and how they relate to your own.

· · · · · · ·

Your health equates to your state of wellness. From a biomedical perspective, historically health was assessed by merely the body's ability to function. While a strong focus on physical wellness (nutrition, hydration, rest, exercise, etc.) still exists today, many perceive health to be more than just what you eat; what you think, say, and do affect your health as well. Health is an integrative interpretation of well-being that encompasses a variety of dimensions—mental, emotional, social, and digital. While a snapshot of one's physical health can aid an assessment of a particular moment, in its totality health cannot be reduced to a singular state. Moreover, prioritizing health requires continued commitment over time. Hence, the practice of promoting soundness of body and mind can foster healthy habits.

A WELLNESS PRACTICE

Investing in boundaries is a health-conscious practice. For someone who is diagnosed with diabetes, for example, boundaries can help to regulate insulin and maintain equilibrium. For someone who is struggling with being disrespected by coworkers, asserting boundaries can help them to promote their social, occupational, and environmental wellness. For someone who is healing through major depression disorder, setting boundaries can help to promote their safety. Artfully crafting and managing boundaries can help to foster your overall well-being.

While the willingness to pay attention to boundaries is an excellent first step, for them to be healthy we need to do more than simply recognize them; we need to see the merit in investing in them. So let's consider some of the aspects of healthy boundaries.

Healthy boundaries tend to resonate deeply. They are representative of what matters most to you. Therefore, when you align with them, this intentional effort converts to congruence, purpose, and authenticity.

Healthy boundaries tend to be a resource for protection. In addition to fostering your well-being, the best of boundaries also safeguard your core self, which includes your personality and integrity. Healthy boundaries are not necessarily one-sided; they are able to protect you and others involved in the boundary as well. For example, when someone who values time divulges this to their partner and establishes personal boundaries around timeliness, clear communication supports both partners. How? The initiating partner gets their boundaries met, and the responding partner is given clear information regarding the other's needs. In addition, the responding partner has been shown how to effectively create a boundary, and in respecting that boundary is able to demonstrate appreciation and support. Further, the responding partner is also able to contribute their perspective on timeliness, seek clarification, or even specify their own needs.

Healthy boundaries tend to be clear. The clarity reduces the amount of space open for misinterpretation and conflict. While boundaries can be deduced by action or inaction over time, the clearest of boundaries are usually explicitly named—via verbal or written communication. For example, if we use the neighbor party reference, over time the neighbors may infer that the lack of friendly exchange might have something to do with their loud parties, and perhaps they would implement a change. However, it's also possible that your lack of doing anything causes them to infer that you are unbothered by the ruckus. Your boundaries might be presumed, or guessed, but the best method, when available, is to clearly communicate them. A key factor that contributes to clarity is consistency. Beyond conveying the boundary, adherence to that boundary helps to reduce confusion for all parties involved. Let's say for example that your digital boundaries have been nonexistent in the past—meaning, you check your messages at all hours, scroll social platforms when you are intended to be sleeping, bury your head in your phone when you're at a social engagement, and/or respond to work communications outside of work hours. However, you decide to establish an evening routine that includes ignoring your devices after 8:00 p.m. In order to support this shift, you decide to convey this new parameter to loved ones and coworkers who are accustomed to receiving communications from you past that time. But if, despite your intentions and your clarified parameter, you continue communicating after 8:00 p.m., your inconsistent adherence in effect nullifies your boundary.

To continue with this example, let's say you take a moment to reassess. Perhaps 8:00 p.m. is unrealistic for you. While it may be something that you hoped for, it may not fit with your life. Your intention to improve digital boundaries can still be maintained by reevaluating the specific time. Learning from what was possible for you, you may consider that digital boundaries are still important, and providing yourself a parameter to disconnect from devices is essential, however, you may opt to choose a later time instead. This process of setting, reflecting on, and editing as needed is paramount in boundary design. Tuning into the process and learning from your mistakes can contribute to a healthy boundary. No person or no boundary is perfect, and nothing is the same forever. It is likely that boundaries will need to be fine-tuned over time in order to meet your needs in the current context. Rather than being stubbornly set in your ways and inappropriately adhering to a boundary that may not serve you, you'll likely find that being open to feedback and willing to reassess will strengthen your boundary-design process.

A healthy boundary does not pertain to a singular person's well-being. The healthiest of interpersonal boundaries consider multiple people in tandem. The goal of protection can be mutually supportive. Take for example boundaries established by newlyweds. While one partner's parameters may not be equivalent to the other's, the compromise and cooperation in the design process supports the marital unit. Even in reference to personal boundaries, investing your energy in crafting individual parameters prompts a natural curiosity of others' boundaries.

Healthy boundaries help to facilitate healing. While forming boundaries is generally helpful sooner than later, there is no deadline on healthy boundary creation. As you learn and heal through the process, you are better equipped to form meaningful parameters. Being able to take your ownership in your healing journey elicits a sense of empowerment. Healthy boundaries help you to acknowledge the doubts that arise as informed by the past, while eliciting hopefulness for the possible transformation that can occur with awareness, dedication, and resilience.

REFLECTION

What misconceptions have you held regarding boundaries? Where do you think those misconceptions come from?

_____

_____

_____

_____

_____

_____

_____

_____

_____

_____

_____

_____

_____

_____

DESIGNING HEALTHY BOUNDARIES

A design is a pattern constructed to implement a specific purpose. The process of designing is often intentional, and is informed by experience and information. Designing often incorporates a balance of specific parameters, originality, and often, a particular style. While we tend to associate design with fields of art and engineering, it can be applied to boundaries as well. Just as a designer's first sketch may not be the exact pattern that becomes the final product, a boundary can be edited in terms of how you apply it, in what context, and whom it applies to.

The entire boundary process serves as a practice of self-respect. As you reflect on which boundaries to set, you acknowledge what matters most to you. As you design those boundaries, you artfully attune to your values and honor yourself by articulating the best ways to protect them. When you remain connected to this purposeful process, you inevitability reap harmony among your thoughts, feelings, values, and actions. When this becomes a common practice, you can find yourself feeling more calm, secure, stable, genuine, confident, happy, and empowered. Further, while all of these benefits can be achieved by personal boundaries alone, the congruence acquired within can then set the stage for advantages in your relationships with others. When you practice self-respect by investing in boundaries, you give others an opportunity to better respect you in turn. Experiencing others respecting your boundaries can help you to feel seen— and, in the best of cases, honored. Healthy connections serve as a great reminder that boundary comprehension and communication do not have to be perpetually draining; instead, they can be an expression of love.

When you foster healthy relationships, the people in your life can help you to see your worth, even in times that you may not. For example, let's say you don't recognize a slip of your own boundary—perhaps you mutter an unkind remark about yourself. A close friend can gently nudge you back to accountability by reminding you that you've been working hard to practice self-kindness and that your remark breaks your own promise. A loved one or a mental health professional can also serve as an extra pair of eyes in situations where you don't realize that someone has bypassed one of your boundaries. In such a moment, that loved one or mental health professional can help you to process this situation, or may even have the opportunity to advocate for you. Furthermore, when you're having trouble understanding, forming, asserting, and healing with boundaries, others who are dedicated to investing in healthy boundaries can serve as an example, can make space for your challenges, and can encourage you throughout the process.

✎ SOURCES OF INSPIRATION

This activity involves seeking sources of inspiration to infuse in your boundary-design journey. This may include past experiences with boundaries of your own or boundaries you have observed (see Reflection on page 14), or what you encountered from your Boundary Hunting (page 14), or you can get creative by including examples from books, movies, and shows. First, list out sources that inspire you. Then, taking each one separately, write it down in the center of a piece of paper and draw a circle around it. Then draw lines out from that circle; at the end of each line, include one detail of why that source inspires you. For example, see the Batman graphic below.

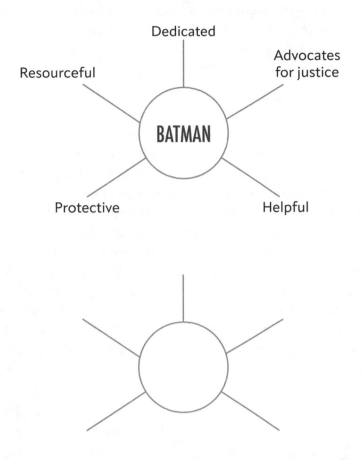

THE STRUCTURE OF HEALTHY BOUNDARIES

This section introduces the framework to cultivate healthy boundary design. You will delve deeper into domains and levels in chapters 5 through 9. Additionally, worksheets to help you explore your domains and levels can be found in the appendix on pages 189, 190, and 191.

BOUNDARY DOMAINS

Boundary domains are the categories in which boundaries may be warranted in your world. They parallel who you are, what you value, what you wish for, and how you choose to live your life. Hence, personal boundaries are often a direct reflection of boundary domains. Also, note that boundaries are not a one-size-fits-all resource. While there may be categories that commonly apply across people, in honoring the uniqueness of every person, that boundary may not appear the same. For example, someone training for a triathlon will likely have different boundaries for rest than someone recovering from surgery—even though their boundaries regarding nutrition and hydration might be similar.

BOUNDARY LEVELS

Boundaries occur on multiple levels. They can be personal or interpersonal. Personal boundaries encompass the parameters that you establish and honor within yourself. Each personal boundary domain has the potential to be further refined by the different roles that you hold. Let's say, for example, that you value honesty. How you define that truthfulness may vary with different people in different contexts, such as a partner at dinner, a colleague in a collaborative meeting, or a child in the hospital. Interpersonal boundaries are those you have with other people, and each domain can vary from one person to the next. For example, your boundaries pertaining to physical touch may differ regarding touch from a partner, another family member, and a stranger. Personal boundaries serve as your core boundaries and provide the basis for peripheral boundaries. Let's say for example that someone highly values mental wellness. Their core boundaries may encompass details such as going to therapy and challenging their unhealthy self-talk. In their relationships, they may intend to cultivate mutual respect and support. On a wider scale, they may try to find environments that do not condone mental health stigmatization or stereotyping.

🗁 PARKER

Let's hear Parker's experience:

If I close my eyes and think of the happiest moments of my life, vivid memories of football come to mind. I see our filled living room on Super Bowl Sunday. I see my mom dropping me off for practice, and a glimpse of everyone I love cheering me on. It is, and has always been, the best part of my life. It helps that I'm good at it, but it's not just about me. Football has always brought my family and friends together. When I look at the stands and see how proud my parents are, there is nothing in the world like it. Knowing that I have the potential to be the first in my family to go to college with a full ride doesn't just make me happy for me, but for my whole family. I'm not good at a lot of things, but when I'm in the game I feel powerful. Coach says if I work hard and play hard I could even have a shot at the pros, and you better bet I'm going to try.

Applying what you've learned in this chapter to Parker's testimony, explore examples for each domain and level in his world, as well as where boundaries may be warranted. For example, one of Parker's domain's is evidently family. In that area, you may suppose that he could benefit from boundaries about how time much time is spent together and how it is spent.

Boundary Domains	Boundary Levels

CHAPTER 2

THREE COMMON OBSTACLES TO CREATING HEALTHY BOUNDARIES

While we all need boundaries, our experiences vary. From my personal and professional work with boundaries, I've noticed that there are three key concerns that impede our ability to have healthy boundaries. Explore each obstacle described to follow, and reflect on if those concerns have affected your journey.

1. OVERLOOKING BOUNDARIES

One major mistake that we often make when it comes to boundary setting is not realizing how essential boundaries are to our well-being. If we experience many of the drawbacks explored earlier, we may not draw the connection to a lack of boundaries being the cause and may fail to see how valuable boundaries could be in our lives. When we don't realize how important boundaries are, it's no surprise that we don't take the time to invest in the process of creating them. Yet the truth is, healthy boundaries often require a substantial amount of time and energy. While the ultimate process often offers the reward of ease, understanding, and harmony, there are times in the process when you can endure the opposite. You may question if the boundary is truly worth the cost. When we initially establish a boundary, going against the grain can be a test of gauging how important the barrier really is for us. For example, a person who is getting accustomed to turning off electronics two hours before bed may toss and turn at first as they adjust to winding down without a TV on. We may consider that a boundary is important but then, after asserting it, the backlash we receive may bring us to second-guess ourselves and potentially back down from upholding it.

Even if we do realize how important boundaries are, we may still miss the mark in evaluating exactly how much time and energy is required to support healthy boundaries. For example, we may aim to establish boundaries, but we may not begin with the prerequisite reflection that is crucial for a sturdy boundary-setting foundation. Without this assessment, we may miss important considerations in our boundary-setting process, such as the purpose of the boundary, who is involved in the boundary, signs that the boundary has been overstepped, and how we can best support the boundary over time.

Another way in which we commonly devalue boundaries is by seeing boundary setting as the entirety of the boundary-management process. We may fall prey to the "set it and forget it" habit of creating boundaries. For example, we recognize that boundaries are important and so we work to create them—but if we fail to realize that the process continues far beyond creation, our initial efforts can eventually fall short. In this realm, we may grow detached from the original intention of establishing the boundary. Over time, we may be less likely to follow the boundary ourselves. In addition, without a firm consistent connection, we may not learn how the boundary can be improved: we may ignore signs that a boundary needs to be enforced—or even cues that it could be loosened.

When we overlook the usefulness of reflection throughout the boundary-setting process, our once-strong boundaries tend to erode. As a result, we can become vulnerable once again. Hence, in addition to setting boundaries, it's essential that we allocate ample energy toward maintaining them. Gaining the full benefit of the overall process calls for setting aside ample time to reflect on it over time.

REFLECTION

Have you bypassed boundaries in the past? If so, explore how this has been helpful or harmful to your process.

_____

_____

_____

_____

_____

2. SKIPPING OVER A FOUNDATION OF SELF-LOVE

When we think about boundaries, we often think about interpersonal boundaries. Of course interpersonal boundaries are part of the healthy boundary-design process, but it's important to note that healthy interpersonal boundaries start with the boundaries we make with ourselves.

At the end of the day, while some of your boundaries may be interpersonal, *all* of them are personal. We often focus on who honors our boundaries—but are we abiding by our own? There are ways that we stand in our own way, yet we may hold the double standard of expecting others to easily honor the exact guidelines that we habitually overlook. If you don't take the time to work on your personal boundaries, your efforts in interpersonal boundaries may falter, which could make your whole venture fruitless.

Contrary to popular belief, boundaries are not intended to help you control others. In fact, they are not even meant to control *ourselves*. Control is an illusion. Similar to the concept of perfection, the concept of having complete control is impossible, and obsessing about how to acquire it can do more harm than good. Think of "perfection" and "control" as being viewed through rose-tinted glasses; they're not realistic. Similarly, boundary design is not a simple sequence of cause and effect. That's because, in any given instance, there are always elements that you cannot account for. For example, designing a boundary rooted in loyalty can help you to highlight that you value honesty, connection, and solidarity. However, it does not mean that you will never be lied to, feel lonely, or experience the end of a relationship. While the purpose of the boundary is valuable, and related methods to assert that boundary may be worthwhile, in actuality there are a variety of variables that can cause things to veer from what's intended. Note, though, that even though we can't employ a control-oriented method, we *can* choose the empowering strategy of a management-oriented method. It's not our responsibility to manage others, but we can do our best to manage ourselves.

Designing healthy boundaries isn't simply about considering ourselves part of the formula; it's also about how we perceive, respect, and care for ourselves in the process. Many times, the reason that others don't or can't successfully honor our boundaries is because we haven't done the same for ourselves. Sometimes this starts by not even knowing what our own boundaries are and why they're important. These details are key to understanding who we are and how we exist in the world. When we don't invest the time to know ourselves, not only are we inevitably vulnerable to triggers, we're also less likely to be able to offer ourselves preventative protection, timely intervention, or compassionate care when friction occurs. Even if we believe we have outlined our boundary, our conflicting attitudes and behaviors can lead to miscommunication and misunderstandings. Instead, it's important to establish a solid foundation of self-love in order to improve healthy boundaries.

We need boundaries for all healthy relationships, and that starts with the one we have with ourselves. When we foster self-love, we honor our intrinsic worth and are better able to accurately assess and assert boundaries, and in turn heal through the boundary process. This includes both the boundaries we set for ourselves in respecting others and those that we set to better honor our own selves.

A key aspect of self-love that influences how we design boundaries is self-respect. When we foster self-respect, we are able to recognize the importance of our boundaries, learn the nuances of how we can align with them, and model how they are to be respected. Then, this provides a framework for others to do the same for us in turn. Reflecting on our intrapersonal boundaries allows us to highlight what is most important and to identify our needs—as well as how we can maintain alignment with these parameters. Further, this awareness and attunement ultimately serves as a foundation for us to better understand interpersonal boundaries, including where they are needed, how to build them, when they are encroached upon, and what to do to maintain them.

Self-love helps you with the foundational recognition that you are worthy of having boundaries. It allows you to visualize the life that you're capable of having with genuine dedication to the process. Self-love assists you in exploring and honoring your true self as you reflect on where boundaries are needed and what they must look like in order to be effective. Self-love also provides a substantial energy source to provide you with fuel for the long, winding path of boundary development. As boundaries can be a challenging process, self-love helps to provide you with encouragement to not only begin but also persist throughout. In addition, self-love provides you with the comfort, grace, and softness that you need in the times that you slip. When you prevail despite the obstacles in your path, self-love helps you to see your resilience, and to utilize it as motivation for the journey ahead. In the times in which you find yourself discouraged from boundary challenges, self-love helps you to validate your pain, remind you of your true intentions, and reroute your path.

Both boundaries and self-love are challenging yet worthwhile endeavors that span throughout the lifetime. Further, as self-love affects boundaries, boundaries affect self-love in turn. We can cultivate self-love throughout the boundary process. When we pay attention to the need for boundaries, we honor our worth. When we explore the variety of boundaries needed to maintain balance in our lives, we validate our needs. When we establish our boundaries, we stake claim in what we are inherently worthy of. When we experience boundary challenges, we give ourselves the ability to reflect, practice humility, and advocate for ourselves. When we tailor our boundaries, we respect our continued growth. Self-love is the often-overlooked element in boundaries that, in reality, fits seamlessly with them, as they are parallel paths.

Have you skipped over setting a foundation of self-love? If so, explore how this has been helpful or unhelpful to your process.

_____

_____

_____

_____

3. OVERUSING BOUNDARIES AS A SYSTEM OF DEFENSE

A variety of missteps can lead us to perceiving boundaries as being solely a method of defense. If we don't have healthy boundaries, we can fall into the trap of utilizing boundaries as a defense system even if we're not necessarily aggressive by nature. That's because even innocent misconceptions can cause boundaries to devolve into militant methods. Earlier we explored that boundaries can be overlooked, but how does this shift from simple oversight to defense mechanism? The formula is pretty straightforward: If we don't value boundaries, we don't set them. However, that doesn't mean that we won't eventually need them.

Having a naïve yet seemingly pacifistic, laissez-faire method to boundaries can actually cause us to be more impulsive and hostile. If we invest in designing healthy boundaries we have the opportunity to access the precious resources for creating them, such as time, reflection, and collaboration. If we lack healthy boundaries, at times when we feel exposed, vulnerable, and even desperate, in a futile effort to protect ourselves we may impulsively assert haphazard boundaries despite our better intentions. Say you start to notice that someone in your social circle tends to make remarks that cross the line. Perhaps you avoid saying anything out of fear of being perceived as overly sensitive, and hope it simply ceases. However, saying nothing can also be received as a kind of tacit approval of such remarks. Over time this unchecked commentary could wear you down—and before you know it you lash out with a regrettable rebuttal that shocks your entire circle, most notably yourself.

When we do recognize that boundaries are important, we may hold a double standard when it comes to personal parameters. In this instance, we may think that we know, and can account for, ourselves; therefore, we may conceptualize that, while boundaries with others are essential, personal boundaries are childish, foolish, and a waste of energy. Have you ever had the experience of realizing there was something you needed to remember (where you placed your phone, what to buy at the grocery store, when to pay your next bill) and you thought to yourself, "I don't need to jot that down, I'm sure to remember"—only to have forgotten soon after? Then you'll know how frustrating it is—not only that you didn't remember, but also that you'd thought about reminding yourself and chose not to. Well, this is somewhat like that. It's hard enough to deal with the challenge at hand; we don't want to also kick ourselves for not investing in ourselves in advance.

It's a myth that mere self-awareness prompts balance. If only it were so simple. Even if this works from time to time in the moments when you're at your best, the humble reality is that you won't always be at your best. Further, that's normal—and therefore to be expected. Also, know that investing in designing personal boundaries doesn't mean that you don't trust yourself. It means you also trust the reality that, as a human being, you will encounter challenges that will keep you from being your best. And so, to better care for yourself, you need to establish bumpers to help you in the future. That's self-trust—the time-travel edition. From this perspective, even seemingly simple boundaries can be used as scaffolding in the future. They can provide support for you from you, and can contribute to your self-love too.

You may see some boundaries with others as more than beneficial, but essential. Because of this dire need, you may misinterpret that the boundary must be blatantly obvious to others. However, if the demarcation isn't clear, it's likely to be crossed at one point or another. For example, two business partners don't discuss where their professional lives end and their personal lives begin. Then at some point one partner wants to hire a family member—and is deeply offended that the other says it's a conflict of interest. To that latter partner, hiring a family member would amount to crossing a boundary. To the other partner, objecting to hiring the family member crosses a boundary. When a boundary is crossed, it can be received as an attack due to both the illusion of clarity and the reality of vulnerability. Even though much of this is due to miscommunication, the encroachment can easily be received as a direct offense. In turn, we may become reactionary and can retort with mismatched force—in order to reinforce a boundary that wasn't clear to begin with.

If we perceive boundaries as a system of defense, sometimes we presume that others see boundaries this way as well. In turn, we may avoid creating boundaries with others due to the fear of how that action will be received—and, subsequently, how we will be perceived. With this in mind, we may worry that discussing boundaries can cause us to seem unkind, selfish, and rude. For example, two friends work for the same employer. One friend copes by talking about work projects outside of work, but the other copes by leaving work at work. If the listener doesn't want to appear to be a bad friend, it may seem like a thoughtful gesture to forgo boundaries altogether. This couldn't be further from the truth. While we may be willing to sacrifice our safety for the potential of keeping the peace, just because we don't set boundaries doesn't mean we won't need them, as noted earlier. And when this happens, if we end up being more impulsive, we become a self-fulfilling prophecy. Our fears of being received as aggressive become a reality because we didn't bother to design healthy boundaries.

COLLABORATIVE BOUNDARIES

Boundary setting is often seen as a one-directional interpersonal process. When we don't perceive boundary establishment as a cooperative venture, an oppositional dynamic begins to surface. We can develop tunnel vision trying to protect ourselves rather than considering how all parties involved can offer mutual respect. Without realizing it, we may villainize the person we're trying to establish a boundary with. In turn, we may unnecessarily increase the rigidity and/or force in which the boundary is established, which can hinder its original intention.

When we feel threatened, it's a natural human response to protect ourselves. When we go into fight-or-flight mode, our bodies prioritize immediate survival over problem-solving. Therefore, in order to prevent slipping into a defensive stance, we must try to work proactively to invest in collaborative boundaries, so we can adopt a proactive, positive perspective. Instead of seeing boundaries as a method of keeping people out, we can see them as an opportunity to deepen connections and let people in.

When self-love is infused into the boundary-design process, the default tactic of defense is replaced with love. In this flipped script, you consider boundaries to be what you welcome, permit, and say "yes" to rather than what you say "no" to. You can honor yourself by creating clear boundaries with yourself as well as with others. With self-love, you value knowing and learning about your needs. In fact, recognizing parameters to protect these needs becomes a natural priority. Therefore, reflecting on boundaries becomes an essential act of love rather than an impulsive strategy of defense. In addition, boundaries may be seen more as a method of connection versus an oppositional dynamic. For personal boundaries, maintaining your recognition and commitment allows you to achieve what you intended—such as happiness, balance, peace, or all of the above. And with interpersonal boundaries, communicating what you need provides an opportunity for others to better understand and care for you. In turn, as others let their guards down, they may share reciprocal boundaries in which you can offer mutual respect. Even in times when friction may arise, a foundation of self-love allows us to weather the ripples, cultivate kindness, and consider the healthiest option to pursue.

REFLECTION

Have you used boundaries as a defense system? If so, explore how this has affected your process.

📁 CORINNE

Corinne had been raised in a financially unstable home. Being one of six with busy parents trying their best to keep the bills paid, she rarely felt seen, much less loved. So she was ecstatic to find herself a classic high school sweetheart; his love was her escape. Soon after graduating they married and started building their family. She found great purpose in making others happy, especially her children. But the more engulfed she became in their lives, the more her marriage began to decline. She didn't realize how far they'd drifted until she caught her husband cheating. The infidelity shook her world. Shortly after, she began to question how often she had been taken for granted, and whether or not she was willing to stand for that anymore.

Now, this is just a snapshot, but let's consider how the three common pitfalls we've covered in this chapter apply to Corinne's situation.

Common Pitfalls	Corrine's Situation
Overlooking boundaries	
Skipping over a foundation of self-love	
Overusing boundaries as a defense system	

CHALLENGES TO DESIGNING HEALTHY BOUNDARIES

Designing healthy boundaries is no easy feat. It takes a lot of time, energy, awareness, and dedication. You may have caught yourself daydreaming about a perfect world in which boundaries wouldn't be needed—no need to think about them, no need to create them, no need to communicate them, no need to fine-tune them, and certainly no need to heal through them. As discussed, perfection is an illusion, and the notion of not needing boundaries is pure fantasy. The diversity of individuals and contexts over time makes boundaries essential. And when boundaries are artfully and intentionally crafted, time spent can be worthwhile, energy can be invigorating, awareness can be valued, and dedication can be rewarded.

Regardless of who you are, you will likely encounter challenges in your boundary journey. A variety of common challenges can crop up as you create, assert, and heal through the process. As we explore each type of challenge, use the exercises in each section to reflect on whether the given challenge has applied to you. If it has occurred in the past, explore how facing that hurdle affected you. If it caused you to retreat, consider what you did not have previously that you could benefit from incorporating into your design process today. If you were triumphant in spite of the hurdle you faced, consider what made that possible, and how those elements can be incorporated into your continued journey.

COMMON FEARS IN THE BOUNDARY-DESIGN JOURNEY

The boundary-design process can elicit concerns. Ranging from slight hesitation to inundating fear, doubts about what the process will entail and what it may provoke can serve as obstacles to designing healthy boundaries. To tend to these emotions, we need to make space for them. Rather than deter them, overlook them, or avoid them altogether, it is important that we instead address them. When we allow ourselves to listen to our boundary-related worries, our underlying questions begin to surface. Taking the time to acknowledge these queries can help us to design healthier boundaries. At the very least, holding space for our fears is an act that infuses self-love into our boundary-design journey. If you're stuck in a fearful thought and then you notice that it's irrational, acknowledging that reality can help to quell that fear. Or, if a thought is unhelpful itself but is informed by a valid trigger, then we may want to allocate energy toward addressing that trigger when designing the boundary itself.

Below is a series of common boundary-related fears that may serve as obstacles in your healthy boundary-design process. These common fears fall within three overarching questions related to ability, commitment, and worth. As you review each section, consider if any of the common worries have applied or currently apply to you.

AM I CAPABLE?

When you learn that creating boundaries is not a one-and-done process, and that even the healthiest of boundaries benefit from being revisited, it is normal to feel a bit intimidated. You may wonder, "Do I have what it takes?" Given you may not have had much exposure to healthy boundary design, it's understandable if you do not feel self-assured in your abilities to design healthy boundaries just yet.

Perhaps you never had the opportunity to witness healthy boundaries designed by others. Even if you have observed boundaries being set, you may not feel adequate to apply the same to your own boundary design. Say for example you witnessed a friend effectively creating a boundary, and then you observed that friend asserting their right to create and hold that boundary. That would be wonderful—but what if you fear that achieving the same result would require a wide area for growth in yourself, something you're not sure you could manage? Further, let's say you've witnessed a family member attempt to form boundaries but then struggle when that boundary wasn't respected—perhaps that boundary was dismissed, or was even met with violence. Being privy to such an experience might deter you from the process altogether.

If you have been fortunate to witness others design healthy boundaries, without personal experience, it is natural to have low boundary-related self-efficacy. Similarly, if you have coura-geously attempted to form a boundary in the past and were met with more challenges than success, it's understandable that you may question your abilities. Even in the scenario in which you set a boundary that you believed was congruent with your needs—if it was not received well by others, and you're uncertain as to why, you may be left disheartened and confused about what to do next. On the other hand, if you were on the receiving end of a new boundary that elicited strong emotions for you, you may be cautious of prompting those emotions in another person, especially if they are close to you.

Or, let's say that, after recognizing your lack of experience with healthy boundaries, you tried to learn more about boundaries. In this process, perhaps you've felt lost and confused; maybe you've struggled to find practical resources to assist in boosting your efficacy. Ultimately, with this continued gap and the raised recognition that boundaries are important, you may feel pressured to set boundaries but fear they'll be ineffective. You may question if you know what's best for you, or if you can successfully assess what you need. Without adequate resources, you may wonder where you will find support for the journey ahead.

REFLECTION

Which of these considerations described above have you experienced in the boundary-design process? Explore how facing these hurdles has affected you. If you retreated, consider what you did not have previously that could benefit you in your design process today. If you were able to persevere, what helped you to persevere? For the questions that apply to you in the present, explore what strengths and areas for growth you have for each.

_____

_____

_____

_____

_____

_____

_____

Do you think you're capable? _____

_____

CAN I COMMIT TO THE PROCESS?

Designing healthy boundaries is not a one-and-done process. Although that would be convenient, the reality is that forming strong boundaries takes quite an investment, one that's much easier said than done. It takes a heightened sense of awareness at the onset, but also requires a refined attunement along the way. Even if you thoroughly reflect and confirm your commitment to forming a healthy boundary, that is merely the beginning. You may have it in you for today, and perhaps tomorrow, but how can you know if you have what it takes to weather the days to come?

Maintenance is a formidable aspect of the healthy-design process; while it may come easy at times, sometimes it takes incremental effort. Similar obstacles that surfaced in setting boundaries can arise after they are formed. If you create a boundary that goes against a well-established tradition, it can be challenging to maintain that boundary—since outside pressure over time can wear down your motivation. Even though your boundaries are intended to guide you toward healthier (often new) habits, it's easy to fall back into familiar patterns. For example, someone who chooses to be sober needs to make that decision on day one and every consecutive day thereafter. But if generational addiction exists in this person's family, and they are the first to choose sobriety, time spent with family can magnetize this individual back into old habits. This can happen even if the other family members aren't pressuring that person to drink with them— just spending time with them can be a challenge.

In times when boundaries are challenged, it can seem draining to need to assess what to do next. Note also that even choosing to withdraw from the boundary-design process altogether comes with its own energetic cost. For example, if after persistent breaches you choose not to loop back to a boundary maintained or enforce your boundary, then you may become vulnerable to continued affronts. Yet, in this time self-love can help you to heal from such breaches and empower you to be your best advocate. It helps to be reminded of the fact that the process of healing is essential to your well-being, and that includes the boundary-development process.

REFLECTION

Which of the above considerations have you experienced in the boundary-design process? Explore how facing these hurdles has affected you. If you retreated, consider what you did not have previously that could benefit you in your design process today. If you were able to persevere, what helped you to persevere? For the questions that apply to you in the present, explore what strengths and areas for growth you have for each.

_____

_____

_____

_____

_____

_____

Do you think you can commit to the process? _____

_____

IS IT WORTH IT?

Considering the energy required to maintain healthy boundaries over time, you may begin to question if it's a worthwhile investment. If you aren't sure of your abilities, would it be better to not try at all? If you're uncertain of your commitment, is it worth starting what you might not be able to continue pursuing? You may think back to your life before the boundary and wonder, "Is it really *that* bad?" You may fall into negotiations with yourself, rationalizing and justifying the status quo.

A key reason you may question if boundaries are worth setting is if you're fearful of the consequences. To begin with, you may wonder how the whole process will affect you. You may wonder, "If I put so much energy into this, will I have time for other priorities? Will I be able to manage going against the grain? What does this boundary mean about *me*?" If you have any negative beliefs about boundaries, you may feel that it would be rude, mean, or cruel of you to form your own boundaries.

Beyond any personal ramifications like the above, you may hesitate to cause undue effects on others. Even the healthiest boundaries can produce friction, personally and interpersonally. If you doubt yourself and the boundary, you may wonder if it will be effective—or if it will cause more harm than good. You may worry that you'll be seen as selfish, mean, or careless. Further, you may not want to cause someone else to feel unseen, unworthy, or unloved. You may find yourself presuming that your boundaries will hurt others. Whereas, the truth is that your boundaries may serve others as well as you.

In addition to not wanting to hurt others, you may fear their reactions. You may question how your boundary will be received. If you fear being rebuked, overlooked, or disrespected, you may consider that abandoning the boundary would be a self-loving method of protection. However, in some instances, abandoning a boundary could risk self-sabotaging your wellness by perpetuating unhealthy dynamics—which themselves do more harm than good. If you recognize that your boundary will likely be met with some degree of antagonism, you may question if you are ready to advocate for yourself. "Am I ready to explain myself? Will I have to fight for myself?" In the worst case, the boundary you form may elicit danger to yourself, others, or all involved. Knowing the potential for risks ahead, you may be uncertain of if you should pursue developing healthy boundaries.

Even if you know deep down that a boundary is worthwhile, external factors can skew your certainty. The healthiest of boundaries can be hard to maintain without a surrounding safe space. Due to the environment, you may not believe that you have the privilege to set the boundary you're worthy of having. When you recognize that your boundary goes against what is common around you, even if you know it's worthwhile, the thought of defending yourself against several people over time can be defeating from the start. For example, consider the plight of a teen (who is secretly gay) who was raised by parents who preached that homosexuality is a sin. As much as that teen might want to be honest and come out to family, friends, and neighbors, the fear of reprisal might make it feel safer to stay silent.

While you may know that a boundary is purposeful for you, when you consider all that you could be up against, you may wonder if it's better to stop before you start. The challenges may stretch beyond your personal realm. Emergencies that throw a wrench in the sturdiest of gates can happen to anyone. Knowing this reality you may question if boundary design would even be worth it. While you cannot prepare for everything, at minimum, well-designed boundaries can serve as a starting point for the times that life pitches a curve ball.

Another reason you may question the value of boundaries is when you assess your odds. If implementing the boundary would risk your receiving consequences from multiple people at the same time, you may feel discouraged in your ability to chart a different path. Even if you believe that change is necessary, when large, established systems have been in place for generations, you may question if your personal crusade could possibly hold a light against what has occurred over time. But remember: Those who have marched in a civil rights protest did so knowing how large the system is that holds that injustice—but that didn't stop them. The hope for change arises out of the unity of multiple voices passionately crying out for change.

REFLECTION

Which of the above considerations have you experienced in the boundary-design process? Explore how facing these hurdles has affected you. If you retreated, consider what you did not have previously that could benefit you in your design process today. If you were able to persevere, what helped you to persevere? For the questions that apply to you in the present, explore what strengths and areas for growth you have for each.

_____

_____

_____

_____

_____

_____

Do you think it's worth it? _____

_____

📁 SAVI

Savi has struggled with self-love for most of her life. Growing up as the youngest in a busy family, she often felt overlooked and questioned her worth. As the years went on, she felt less and less comfortable in her own skin, especially when around others. Her family never noticed any signs of her struggle as she always kept to herself—other than a self-deprecating quip that would slip out from time to time. She tried her best to cope, but never felt comfortable asking for help—or even asking any questions. Then, in high school she started experimenting with drugs. Deep down she was always scared to use and tried quitting a few times—but since it seemed to be the only thing that helped her escape her sadness and anxiety, she couldn't stop. In her senior year she sneaked out to a college party with a couple of her friends. This turned out tragically, because she was attacked. Though Savi got safely home, she started blaming herself from the moment she opened her eyes the next day. While most of the night was a blur, what she did remember were brief flashes of that trauma. She couldn't imagine a single positive outcome of telling someone, so, like the rest of her challenges, she chose to keep it to herself. Feeling more out of control than ever before, she made a promise to herself to never use ever again.

Applying what you've learned in this chapter to the above scenario, highlight some of Savi's fears about boundaries. Then, consider what she may need in order to work through those fears and design healthy boundaries.

_____

_____

_____

_____

_____

_____

· · · · · · ·

COMMON REASONS WHY BOUNDARIES ARE HARD TO RECEIVE

As challenging as it can be to set boundaries, they can also be challenging to receive. This fact can be very discouraging. Exploring what makes a boundary challenging to receive can help you to refine your boundary design. Delving deeper to consider your difficulties with receiving boundaries, and the times others have had trouble receiving your boundaries, can be informative considerations in designing healthy boundaries.

BOUNDARIES CAN BE CHALLENGING TO RECEIVE WHEN THEY'RE NEW

It can be challenging to receive a boundary at any time, but it can be especially so when the boundary is new. Just as boundaries can call for ample time in the formation process, we must also be patient in the reception process as well. And some boundaries may take longer to adjust to than others. While some boundaries may be understood quickly, the practice of aligning with them may take time. Adjusting to a new boundary may require some retraining of the brain, since a previous pattern may be in place that warrants time and intention to be overwritten. For example, someone who wants to establish a habit of exercising after work may find themselves consistently forgetting to pack their workout gear. Given that they're trying to form a routine, they might find that forgetfulness frustrating, but it doesn't necessarily indicate that they actually resist establishing a new regimen.

BOUNDARIES CAN BE CHALLENGING TO RECEIVE WHEN THEY ARE UNCLEAR

Boundaries are difficult to receive—or perceive—when it isn't clear that they exist in the first place. It could be that the parameter was not directly, or thoroughly, conveyed. It could also be that the recipient struggled to listen or understand. Even if the boundary was clear initially, inconsistency around it could cloud it over time. For example, someone can set parameters around criticizing others, yet make self-deprecating comments. Another person may announce they wish to avoid gossip, but then talk behind an acquaintance's back.

Even if the boundary itself is clearly stated, if its importance, conditions, or consequences are left unknown, a misunderstanding could ensue. And while any boundary worth setting warrants respect, if it is also conveyed that the bound is of grave importance, theoretically a recipient would be more inclined to honor it. For example, if a friend told you they were healing through an alcohol addiction, you wouldn't bring champagne to their housewarming.

A common misconception is presuming that boundaries are set to protect someone from specific people—namely, those who are dangerous, untrustworthy, or malicious. In other words, sometimes boundaries aren't received because an intended recipient may assume that the boundary doesn't apply to them. Often due to a perception of closeness, this person may infer that they are granted a special access pass even when that's not the case. For example, Nellie recently endured a difficult breakup. Shortly after, she shared with her loved ones that she was not ready to talk about it. However, her best friend texted her, called her—and even showed up at her door when she didn't hear from her. The friend assumed that Nellie's request didn't apply to her and presumed that Nellie needed her support.

On the other hand, if the recipient is more peripheral, they may not feel comfortable asking clarifying questions to better understand the boundary, thus increasing the risk of not comprehending it in its entirety. Returning to Nellie's situation, let's say that, despite what she said, she actually did need support after her breakup. Her best friend showing up at her door might be exactly what she needed. Whereas, peripheral friends might hesitate to offer support due to uncertainty of her wishes.

BOUNDARIES CAN BE CHALLENGING TO RECEIVE WHEN THEY EVOKE UNPLEASANT EMOTIONS

Boundaries can be received warmly. When you honor a boundary, you may feel content, fulfilled, or proud. When a supportive person receives your boundary well, you can both feel respectful and respected. However, since boundaries are more often than not seen as a method of defense, they can evoke unpleasant emotions, which can impede effectiveness. In terms of personal boundaries, setting a boundary for you from you can make you question what that means about you. Say for example you need to set a boundary to cap the number of drinks you consume at a dinner. Setting this boundary may elicit emotions of confusion, disappointment, and perhaps even shame. For others, when a boundary is misinterpreted, they can feel annoyed, offended, or hurt. In turn, their negative reception can provoke your own. You may fear that setting the boundary means you are unkind, inconsiderate, or even aggressive. The truth is, even the healthiest of boundary designs can be received poorly. Because much is left to context, a boundary in which you hold positive sentiments still carries the risk of someone feeling disrespected or unloved. Boundaries can trigger a breadth of emotions; unfortunately, if we are unwilling to acknowledge these feelings and directly discuss boundaries, we increase the odds of the boundaries being poorly received.

BOUNDARIES CAN BE CHALLENGING TO RECEIVE WHEN THEY CAUSE FRICTION

Setting boundaries can cause friction. Even if it's a boundary you formed for yourself, it may not necessarily come with ease. Readiness, patience, and accountability are key in moderating friction. Habits form over time and take time to break as well. While your heart may be in the right place, it takes much more than good vibes to establish a boundary. It is natural for a boundary to cause you to question yourself—including your intentions, motivation, and even your identity. As you continue, the recognition of the boundary, including its value and your worth, will help to reduce the friction over time. Think back to the example of the person who wants to exercise after work yet consistently forgets to pack their gear. After a few consecutive days of forgetting, they may question if their intention to exercise after work is sound. With self-love that person could acknowledge that they may need help to surpass the friction of forgetfulness. If they reiterate that this intention to exercise is important, they may employ additional strategies to make it happen, such as setting a reminder to pack their gym bag the night prior and then placing it at the front door.

Boundaries can also ignite friction with others. While the parameter may be new, the world in which it is placed is not. Many systems predate the boundary, and many people are accustomed to the open space that the boundary now overtakes. Let's take for example new parents establishing their family culture with the birth of their child. Despite their excitement to have their loved ones meet their little one, the couple decides to heed their doctor's advice to keep their infant home and to receive few visitors in the early weeks. Just as it can take time for you to adjust to a new boundary, the same applies for others. This can be particularly challenging when the boundary conflicts with others' thoughts, beliefs, patterns, behaviors, feelings, hopes—or boundaries of their own. The new parents' preferences may cause friction for loved ones eager to meet the newborn, and may even go against long-established cultural norms for extended family members, religious leaders, and close friends, who might wish to shower the baby with affection and protection in the early days. The mismatch can cause the recipient to feel confused, intimidated, and/or offended. It can also internalize: the friction can morph into the person questioning their reality, including their intentions, beliefs, behaviors, and feelings. Oftentimes boundary friction between two people is a projection of an internal threat of how someone views themself, the relationship, or even the world.

Friction can amplify when the boundary goes against what many others have held firm over time. As a simple equation, the pressure increases when the boundary conflicts with numerous people. Interpersonal friction in the boundary-design process often applies to boundaries that challenge customs, traditions, and regulations that have been upheld for generations. This type of friction can be seen as a challenge, as though calling into question all that the people involved believe to be valid, important, and true. And so, if someone doesn't instantly receive your boundary with warmth it doesn't necessarily mean that they don't wish to; conflict that is addressed with care, patience, and compassion can be resolved successfully—and even strengthen a relationship.

While friction has the potential to deter the healthy boundary-design process, it can be redirected if you broaden your perception of it. No two people are the same. Even those who are close to us or similar to us still have differences in preferences, opinions, and perspectives. Instead of seeing friction as a tactic of defense, you can acknowledge that it is a natural occurrence when there is a mismatch between worldviews. Normalizing the occurrence of friction removes unnecessary blame and reduces the risk of the slippery slope toward unwarranted aggression. The traditional method of boundary formation can demonize those who react defensively to our boundaries. However, not all who push on our boundaries are malicious. When we take the time to consider from where friction arises, and how easily it can arise, we can see the humble reality of how easily we can unintentionally initiate friction with others. We may all be the culprit at one time or another. Also, note that, though there may be instances when you need to firmly advocate for your boundaries, it's not likely that this will be required at *every* sign of friction.

📁 DAVE AND RAE

Dave has been dating Rae for a few months. He enjoys their many similarities, ease of communication, and shared interests. He decides to delete his dating apps and stop talking to other potential matches. Dave then decides to share his feelings, hoping that Rae is equally interested in developing their relationship further. To his surprise, Rae confesses that, while they're compatible on paper, they lack chemistry and intimacy. Rae says it would be best for them to go their separate ways sooner rather than later.

Applying what you've learned in this chapter to the above scenario, explore why it may be challenging for Dave to receive Rae's boundary.

_____

_____

_____

_____

_____

_____

_____

_____

_____

_____

REFLECTION

Think about a time when you may have struggled to receive a boundary. Was this a personal or interpersonal parameter? What happened? How did you react? What emotions did you experience throughout the process? Which of the common obstacles in receiving a boundary played a role in this experience?

_____

_____

_____

_____

_____

_____

_____

_____

_____

_____

_____

_____

_____

_____

It's important to note that, while we can get offended when others push our boundaries, we may not realize the ways we push others' parameters (or even our own). Developing greater awareness of this dynamic can help us shift from a defensive mindset of boundary design to a collaborative, even loving framework. We can't be responsible for others' reactions, but we can design healthier boundaries. We can do this by being mindful about how boundaries are received, being cognizant about what may influence how they're received, and being humble in the recognition that anyone, even with the best intentions, could struggle to receive a boundary at some point. Acknowledging this reality can help us to be more compassionate, both with ourselves when we infringe on our personal boundaries, and with others when they push on ours.

So let's return to the practice example above. Rae set a boundary by telling Dave their feelings didn't quite mutually align, and Dave struggled to receive Rae's boundary. Beyond the initial shock of the stark contrast in their feelings, he hoped they could continue to be friends. He continued to contact Rae throughout the following week, and was disappointed when his messages got no reply. By the end of that week, Rae clarified it would be best if they cut communication altogether. To this Dave experienced a storm of emotion, from confusion for why, resentment for wasting his time, sadness for losing the relationship, and anger at the abrupt ending without considering his emotions.

Recall that Dave had stopped interacting with other people in the dating apps before he shared his feelings with Rae. In his flurry to deepen their relationship, it hadn't occurred to him how he'd often been in a position similar to Rae's. Dave had ghosted one person entirely; with another he'd canceled a date via text at the last minute. In both those situations, he hadn't considered the others' feelings. In times of friction, it's helpful to not only put yourself in someone else's shoes, but also consider the times you were in a similar scenario. Practicing empathy and sympathy can help highlight areas of friction as well as illuminate how they can be ameliorated.

CHAPTER 4

SETTING BOUNDARIES WITH SELF-LOVE

For the purpose of this guide, self-love is broadly defined as the active practice of accepting, caring for, and encouraging oneself. It encompasses both the love that comes from within you and the love that you give to yourself. The process of self-love begins with the mere task of being able to appreciate you for you. It is crucial to be kind and considerate toward yourself; however, self-love is more than a sentiment. Beyond your ability to tend to yourself, you must remember that self-love is an intentional practice to learn and cultivate.

Designing healthy boundaries is grounded in *self*-love. Hence, the method offered in this book will help you to better understand your individual lens. While others and society will be considered, the primary focus will be on you. From time to time, especially in challenging moments, it may feel like there is heavy emphasis on the self even when there are other factors to consider beyond you. When this pressure becomes distracting, allow yourself to take a break from the process. The redirected focus to the self is not intended to blame yourself as a victim or foster self-deprecation; in actuality, the intention is exactly the opposite. When you thread self-love throughout the boundary-design process, the focus loops back to your perspective to empower you. Your boundaries may be affected by the world you exist in, but they start with you.

Similarly, while the term "self-love" quite literally begins with *self*, it by no means ends that way. A common misconception about self-love is that it entails a love solely for yourself. Self-love is not to be confused with narcissism. In fact, one of the main reasons to invest in self-love is that it will assist you in better caring for others too. Think about it: Would you be better able to give energy to someone when you're stressed, inundated, burned out, and neglectful of your needs—or when you're balanced, present, rested, and energized?

Inherent to the "self-love" phrase itself, the process of loving oneself is ultimately a subjective experience. And while external influences are common, the resilience to consistently invest, refine, and—when needed—protect our boundaries comes from our inner power. How it is defined, what it may look like, and how it tends to be deterred differs from person to person. Additionally, although it is helpful to bond through mutual support from others who are like-minded, caring, and on similar journeys, at the end of the day the overall effectiveness of the boundary process is heavily dependent on personal effort. For that reason, when we wish to delve deeper into this journey, it is important to take time to reflect on what self-love means to us personally.

REFLECTION

How do you define self-love? What key words come to mind? Can you think of a time when you felt your self-love was strong?

Self-love provides you with the opportunity to see yourself completely, to recognize your strengths and weaknesses, triumphs and challenges. It is critical to acknowledge your areas for growth and the obstacles in your path in order to inform your boundary preparation, creation, assertion, and healing.

Self-love is wondrously empowering and validating, yet it's not always an easy task. It's more than indulging in your favorite food and escaping to an island paradise. Within this process, it is helpful to recognize that without darkness there cannot be a sincere appreciation for light. Self-love also requires the courage to reflect on where you are, the bravery to consider where you want to be, and the tenacity to strive to be a better version of your true self.

Just as we often think of boundaries as being only an interpersonal process, and may overlook how essential intrapersonal parameters are, we tend to perceive love as being only an exchange between people, and may overlook how love can also be a force from you to you. In reality, we need love from ourselves, and boundaries with ourselves, in order to live a healthy life—and to have healthy relationships with others. Assess your present self-love with The Seven Segments of Self-Love on page 188.

WHY SELF-LOVE IS CRUCIAL IN THE BOUNDARY PROCESS

When it comes to designing healthy boundaries, self-love isn't optional, it's crucial. In order to design effective boundaries, before you even consider taking any action you must believe in yourself. Self-love shows you that boundaries are valuable, that you're worthy of them, and that you're capable of cultivating them. It is the essence of self-love that helps you to unlock the ability to engage in the boundary process. Further, self-love helps you to recognize and understand your truest self, and this self-knowledge assists in informing meaningful boundaries.

Just as self-love is a continuous journey, investing in healthy boundaries will persist throughout your lifetime. As you design and maintain healthy boundaries, self-love can serve as a reminder that you are worthy of balance, happiness, and protection. Hence, maintaining the connection between crafting boundaries and self-love helps to foster the motivation, courage, and dedication necessary to provide purposeful parameters over time.

Self-love reminds us that perfection isn't possible. From this perspective, we require humility to acknowledge that hard work, dedication, and courage—often the form of multiple efforts—are what we can expect when designing healthy boundaries. As solid as our demarcations may seem to us, there are a variety of variables beyond our control, such as what others believe and how they will react. Further, we all have blind spots, and there may be things about our own selves that we can't fully account for in the process. Instead of stubbornly fighting to control what is beyond our realm of control, our energy can be better used by seeing such moments as space to improve.

As time passes, the world around us—and the contexts we find ourselves in—constantly change. While there are often consistencies within ourselves, such as our values, we also shift over time. This doesn't mean that we are fickle. Change is inevitable. Not only is this natural and normal, in the best of cases it also can be a sign that we're learning and growing. With this being said, even if we've designed the best boundaries possible for the present moment, it's important to acknowledge that part of the process is revisiting, reassessing, and potentially revising those boundaries, too. When this happens, we can give ourselves the love we need by being flexible and embracing the process.

Self-love offers us an empowering base from which to design our boundaries. We can't control others, or the world around us—therefore, we are not responsible for what's beyond our realm.

However, we can recalibrate our focus to better manage ourselves. At the end of the day, all boundaries are personal. Establishing a solid, subjective foundation can help to inform our boundaries with others. And when your boundaries falter, and you feel shaken in the process, this stability can be where you return to. Self-love helps us to find our center, and through that portal we can better connect with who we are and what we need.

REFLECTION

Think about three boundary conflicts you have experienced. How does self-love factor into these concerns?

_____

_____

_____

_____

_____

_____

_____

_____

Self-love comes with a wealth of benefits, but often they do not come easily. To begin, it can be challenging to foster self-love if we don't believe we are worthy. We may hold self-disparaging beliefs that block us from even convincing ourselves self-love is possible, let alone that we should invest in the process. On top of that, much of our disbelief can be influenced by the world around us. If we were raised in families that didn't reinforce our worth, or in communities that challenged our worth, or in societies that devalued our worth, it can be difficult to fathom that we are worthy—and worthy of self-love. Parents who pressure, classmates who jeer, and partners who cheat can all contribute to our sense of worth—as do airbrushed advertisements that insinuate we're not enough just as we are.

Love is a core human need, but when physiological safety is challenged, it may feel like a luxury. When we're in a dangerous environment, it can be difficult, and potentially even harmful, to fixate on self-love. Dealing with the fear of active violence, such as from an abusive partner or a societal threat, can understandably skew our focus to prioritize survival. Unfortunately, those who experience this on a regular basis find it even harder to invest in self-love.

Even when we're able to confront self-defeating thoughts, stand up against harmful messages, and reap the privilege of a safe environment, self-love can still be challenging. In addition to internal and external pressures, self-love takes a lot of continuous energy. But the process of self-love is not a summit to conquer; it is a continuous practice of caring for yourself. Hence, self-love includes the dedication to prioritize yourself regardless of what life may bring.

THE SEVEN SEGMENTS OF SELF-LOVE

To better elucidate self-love and why it's a prerequisite to boundary design, it can be helpful to understand the seven segments of self-love. As you review each section, reflect on how you have already strengthened each area—and where you find opportunities for growth. If possible, try to cite a specific example for each. You might also find it helpful to refer to The Seven Segments of Self-Love worksheet in the appendix on page 188.

SELF-AWARENESS

Self-love requires your attention. It necessitates a willing introspection to help you better understand your thoughts, feelings, desires, motives, and overall self. Your reflection equips you with the ability to promote your well-being by being conscientious and engaged. Self-awareness allows you to recognize when you're in need of self-love and when you're actively fostering self-love. This aspect of self-love is often overlooked, as it seems rudimentary—but the simplicity of being willing to notice the world around you, and to see how it influences the world within you, is a critical component to deepening self-love.

When self-awareness is lacking, our conceptualization of boundaries may be cloudy and confusing. We may recognize we need some semblance of boundaries, but we cannot clearly discern where they are needed, why they are needed, and what they need to look like. With this uncertainty, we cannot design healthy boundaries for ourselves, much less with anyone else.

In chapter 2 we explored three common pitfalls to boundary setting. As you may recall, one problem is that we often devalue boundaries. Without self-awareness, we may not even recognize that we need boundaries. When we don't reflect—or even notice that we need time to reflect—it becomes difficult to realize where and when boundaries are needed. When boundaries are overlooked in this way, we become vulnerable to the consequences of lacking protective parameters.

Self-awareness can serve your boundary-design process at each step of the journey. When you're creating boundaries, self-awareness allows you to better see yourself in order to know where boundaries are needed, whom you need them with, and why they're important. When you're asserting your boundaries, self-awareness helps you to take note of your experiences in the process. Once you develop this skill, you can swiftly recognize when boundaries are being challenged and alter them as needed. When boundaries are violated, self-awareness supports you in recognizing what your foundational needs are. Moreover, self-awareness helps you to reflect on your role throughout the process—including taking accountability and celebrating your growth—and helps you to incorporate learned lessons from one boundary to the next.

Boundaries are nuanced. Your boundaries may have core concepts that remain consistent over time, but even the best-designed boundary won't last you a lifetime. Contexts shift, and people change. Being self-aware helps you to attune to these differences and recognize when your structures may warrant revisiting as well.

Self-awareness helps you to recognize both challenges and what may be required to tackle them. In fact, a refined sense of self-awareness can even help you to anticipate hurdles before you reach them, thus allowing you to adequately prepare. Even when a difficulty catches you off-hand, self-awareness helps you to reconnect, reflect, and recognize the best next steps for boundary-maintenance and healing.

Though boundaries don't need to be formed individually, each individual must actively engage in their boundary-design journey. Also, as previously noted, while it can be resourceful to witness others' effective processes in action, since every person is unique and contexts vary, what works for someone may not necessarily work for you. Self-awareness allows you to embrace this reality while using insight from sources of inspiration to design healthy boundaries.

REFLECTION

In what ways has your self-awareness strengthened over time? What opportunities might you take to cultivate self-awareness in the future?

SELF-EXPLORATION

Self-exploration encompasses the courage to improve your self-knowledge. This requires the willingness to educate yourself about who you are—not just on the surface, but at your core. While self-love benefits all, it's not a one-size-fits-all process. What works for someone may not work for another. Since you can't simply copy and paste someone's progress/methodology, you have to put in the personal effort to learn about who you are, what matters to you, and how you want to make the most out of your life.

Without self-exploration, your good intentions of boundary setting could be met with haphazardly formed boundaries. This can cause us to invest energy in the wrong places, which inevitably means having to revisit the boundaries more often, and ultimately having to use more energy over time.

When it comes to boundaries, self-awareness is just the tip of the iceberg. Tethered to your identity, self-exploration helps you to understand both what you wish to protect and your underlying motivations. When you're willing to reflect deeply you're able to see your truth, including where boundaries are warranted, which ultimately improves your intentionality in boundary design. With this deepened connection, you're able to set meaningful parameters. Further, being tethered to your purpose fuels ambition for your continued boundary journey. Consider a couple planning for marriage. If they are both connected to who they are, what they value, and how they find balance as individuals, this helps them both to first decide if marriage is suitable for them as people, and also if their partner would be a compatible spouse in the long-run. Further, knowing these tenets essentially become their marital vows, which can help them to be aligned throughout the course of their marriage.

Self-exploration helps us to assess our wellness. It is resourceful in discerning when you have the capacity to reflect and set boundaries. It can assist you in aptly choosing whether to step up and advocate or walk away and heal.

When we embrace self-exploration we are able to be honest with ourselves as well as others. This encompasses the ability to receive feedback and make space for varied perspectives—both of which are resourceful in boundary design. Self-exploration allows you to hold space for your lived experience as well as that of others. Values, identity, balance, and growth will all look different from person to person. Simply explore that all perspectives can be valid. For example, not every instance in which a boundary is pushed is representative of an intentional strike. There are times when a boundary may be unrecognized. Additionally, someone who is distracted or overwhelmed may unintentionally overlook your boundary. While this does not necessarily qualify as an excuse, if you maintain an exploratory mindset you can empathize and understand. These qualities can assist you in choosing boundary-healing over pure defense.

Boundaries warrant maintenance. Over time, some require fine-tuning, and others require changing altogether. Approaching this reality from a stance of curiosity can encourage you in your continued path. Further, when you adopt the perspective of being a lifetime learner, you're able to integrate feedback to inform strengthened boundaries over time.

In what ways has your self-exploration strengthened over time? What opportunities might you take to cultivate self-exploration in the future?

_____

_____

_____

_____

_____

_____

_____

SELF-CARE

Self-care is the continuous process of proactively considering and tending to your needs in order to cultivate your wellness in the present. It is a holistic process that we all need in order to foster presence, engagement, self-love, and boundaries. Self-care is not a singular skill. Instead, self-care includes a wide variety of tasks tailored to meet your diverse needs. Although there may be similarities between self-care strategies—like the broader concept of self-love—self-care is subjective and tends to vary from person to person. Generally speaking, having a diverse set of coping skills to utilize when we're off-kilter can help us maintain our equilibrium.

Without self-care you are at risk of lacking the energy to design healthy boundaries. Without the intentional practice of self-care, when we are lacking in an integral aspect of our wellness, our energy will be pulled from present resources and strengths. While this may temporarily suffice, over time, what was a strength can diminish due to overdependence. A simple example is if you catch a cold. Your physical wellness will be a priority and others such as social, occupational, or financial take a back seat. If you typically practice holistic self-care, such as by being on top of your work tasks, budgeting your finances, and staying connected with your loved ones, the pull of wellness from those areas will be okay in that interim.

If we experience burnout, our well-being needs to be prioritized. That calls for first setting boundaries that cultivate balance so that other healthy boundaries can be formed and followed. Since healthy boundary design is a continuous process, our success is dependent on our being well rested and balanced. Without adequate self-care, we may not have the energy to support even our personal boundaries—which in turn support our interpersonal boundaries.

Boundary design can be a helpful fabric to weave into your comprehensive self-care. Well-formed boundaries can help you establish what is important to you and can help you ultimately cultivate wellness. In addition, self-care helps you to manage your well-being and calibrate toward equilibrium throughout the ongoing boundary journey. And while consistent self-care supports healthy boundaries, it's especially warranted when your boundaries are disregarded, since self-care can help you regain your balance. As you likely can imagine, there is a symbiotic connection between boundaries and self-care. When we practice self-care, we have the energy, awareness, flexibility, and motivation to design and maintain our boundaries. When our boundaries are designed well, with time our self-care becomes second nature, and we reap the benefits of enhanced wellness.

REFLECTION

In what ways has your self-care strengthened over time? What opportunities might you take to cultivate self-care in the future?

SELF-ESTEEM

Self-esteem encompasses how you appraise your worth. Your view of yourself in turn influences how you think, feel, and act. Your overall assessment has a variety of components, including how you see your ability to perform a certain task as well as your trust in your abilities. In addition, your general perceptions tend to be influenced by your experiences, personality, culture, and the current context. And while low self-esteem is related to poor mental wellness, that doesn't necessarily mean that high self-esteem is the pinnacle either. Inflated self-esteem can cause problems of its own, such as lack of awareness or empathy. Moderate self-esteem keeps us centered and grounded, and allows us to recognize our worth *alongside* the worth of others. We are not better than; we are just as worthy.

How you appraise your worth affects how you design boundaries. Negative views can impede your ability to recognize where you need boundaries, whether you are worthy of protecting your peace, what you need to do, and how you play an important part in the process. Inflated self-esteem may mean you are missing perspectives, such as your personal blind spots or others' lived experiences. Without a moderate sense of self-esteem, you may not hold balanced views of yourself, and this may skew your boundary-design process.

When we have a healthy sense of self-esteem we feel encouraged to invest in necessary boundaries and are welcoming of others doing the same. When boundaries are not received well by others, a healthy sense of self-esteem helps to buffer the challenge. It also enables us to let go of feeling responsible for how others respond; instead, we are grounded in our personal reference, assessment, and truth. When we cultivate self-esteem, we are able to feel more connected and confident in our worth, purpose, and intentions.

When we have a healthy sense of self-esteem, we are able to design boundaries that consider ourselves as well as others. As noted throughout this book, boundary design is not an easy process. Boundaries can be daunting to form, difficult to maintain, and intimidating to defend. But when we effectively manage boundaries, we can take pride in knowing we are successful in recognizing our needs, communicating our conditions—and staying centered in the process.

REFLECTION

In what ways has your self-esteem strengthened over time? What opportunities might you take to cultivate self-esteem in the future?

SELF-KINDNESS

Self-kindness is the skill of being friendly to yourself. It is the gentleness, comfort, and love you offer yourself—when times are challenging as well as when times are joyous. Your inner dialogue is informed by a variety of factors, such as your personality, your experiences, and the people in your environment. Oftentimes, people are kinder to others than they are to their actual selves. Further, many people would never speak to others the way their inner critic speaks to them—yet never realize their hypocrisy. As you can see, while we can understand the utility of self-kindness theoretically, we can have a harder time putting it into action. And while components of kindness are simple, the practice of self-kindness often takes a great deal of effort. Support from others is certainly helpful, but even the most encouraging environments can fall short when we're unable to be kind to ourselves. It is as if others are pouring into our cup without realizing there is a hole at the bottom of it.

When your self-talk is riddled with self-criticism over self-kindness, you may face a variety of boundary struggles. One, you may not even set necessary boundaries—since boundaries are an act of self-kindness. Two, even once you do form boundaries, you may not effectively assert them; you may become distracted by unhealthy self-talk, such as, "I'm not good at setting boundaries," "There's no point in setting boundaries because nothing will change," and "This boundary is going to ruin my relationship." Lastly, even if you do assert your boundaries, you may not immediately notice when they are encroached—since someone else's lack of kindness wouldn't stand out from your own inner unkindness.

When you face boundary challenges, regardless of whether they occur in the creating, asserting, or healing phase, self-kindness helps you to care for yourself in the journey. Throughout the process you are likely to experience a wealth of emotions, such as being apprehensive of delving into boundaries, fearful of laying a boundary, disappointed when you surpass your own boundary, or even rage when someone bypasses your boundary—for what seems like the thirty-seventh time. In order to persist despite the challenges in the boundary-design journey, you must be kind to yourself. This gentle support will enable you to treat yourself well and will pave the path for you to not be just your own friend, but also your own advocate.

Self-kindness allows you the patience necessary for the long haul. At the onset, you're able to offer yourself adequate time and space to reflect. With self-kindness, you recognize that you cannot rush the process of boundary assertion. Instead of hastily and haphazardly setting boundaries, you are able to pace your progress. These steady strides allow you to immerse in the process such that you're able to catch and absorb the lessons available to you. Rather than internalizing the struggles of the boundary-design process, you're able to offer yourself the grace and compassion needed to heal.

Self-kindness helps you to humbly embrace the ups and downs of boundary design. It can help you to persevere throughout the process of revisiting and fine-tuning boundaries. It permits you to accept the reality that boundaries often evolve, and that you are not to be blamed or shamed for having to revisit your parameters. Rather than seeing hurdles as blatant discouragement, with self-kindness you're able to recognize that obstacles are a part of the boundary-design journey. In addition, when in the thick of a challenge, you're able to offer yourself much-needed support to persevere.

In what ways has your self-kindness strengthened over time? What opportunities might you take to cultivate self-kindness in the future?

_____

_____

_____

_____

_____

_____

_____

_____

SELF-RESPECT

Blossoming out of admiration, respect is demonstrated by acknowledging a person's dignity. As a basic human right, we are all worthy of respect. We are all equal. You are deserving of respect from others and from yourself as well. While respecting others is honorable, continually prioritizing respect of others at the expense of our own needs is not a self-loving act. Moreover, this well-intentioned negligence can be dangerous to your mental health, and potentially detrimental to your relationships as well. A strong sense of self-respect helps you to better respect others and to be better respected by others. The respect you deserve is neither more nor less than that of anyone else; all is essential.

When self-respect is lacking, you risk disproportionately investing in the boundary-design process. Knowing who you are, what matters to you, and why are key components of both self-respect and of designing healthy boundaries. Without these anchors, you may understand the importance of boundaries but may pour energy into the wrong places, inevitably leading to purposeless, poorly designed parameters. To build upon the example of the couple considering marriage on page 49, one partner might realize that they don't actually value marriage. Not taking the time to recognize that they value long-term commitments yet not marriage can cause them to pour into a relationship in which their partner and community pressure marriage over time.

If you do not practice respect with yourself, you may be unfamiliar with what authentic respect looks like. In turn, you may not notice when others are pushing on your boundaries and when advocacy is warranted. You may aimlessly demand respect from others but may lack a basis for yourself. On the other hand, when someone does offer genuine respect, it may feel foreign and unfamiliar, causing you to doubt the boundary altogether.

Boundaries play an essential role in promoting and preserving self-respect. The mere decision to design boundaries is an act of self-love, as choosing to do so honors your worth and dignity. When self-respect is cultivated, we are more aware of what matters most to us and we are keen to learn how to protect those areas. Self-respect begins with your treatment of yourself then helps you to establish a strong foundation for all boundaries. Honoring your own boundaries models how others can do the same in respecting you. As you honor your unique needs, you encourage others to honor your needs and make space for them to honor their own boundaries as well.

REFLECTION

In what ways has your self-respect strengthened over time? What opportunities might you take to cultivate self-respect in the future?

SELF-GROWTH

No one is perfect, and no one will ever be. Further, as time passes we change, and the world around us transforms as well. When we acknowledge the intersection of these realities, we access the opportunity to embrace the role of being a lifetime learner. This humbling perspective can also empower us to accept that there will always be room for growth. When we aren't hyper-focused on a particular finish line far off on the horizon, we gain the widened perspective of acknowledging the beauty of the present, how far we have come, and where we can continue to go. Hence, self-love becomes a process in which we continually seek opportunities to learn, love, and thrive.

Without a growth mindset, the boundary-design journey will be a bit more challenging. To start with, we may lack enthusiasm about boundaries and their subsequent benefits if we don't acknowledge that they can help us to grow. In addition, the perpetual process will seem discouraging and depleting rather than encouraging and rewarding. And when we encounter obstacles, we may perceive them as a reflection of our failure—or, worse, we may internalize the hurdle, deeming ourselves a failure.

The perspective that we can grow throughout our life parallels the reality that boundaries are essential throughout our lifetime. As a result, they require active time, energy, and dedication. When we embrace this truth, we release the notion that boundaries are a one-and-done process. Instead, creation, assertion, and healing all offer lessons about ourselves, others, and the world. In addition, each boundary experience informs another. Therefore, during the continued chance to learn, we improve our awareness, abilities, and self-love.

Infusing a growth mindset into the boundary-design process allows us to see ourselves wholly—strengths and opportunities for growth alike. Strengths are not merely utilized, but celebrated. This is especially true when dedication to growth earns us a new skill, lesson, or resource. What would otherwise have been perceived as weakness is instead welcomed as areas for growth. The ability to grow humbly acknowledges that our growth can be best supported with the aid of others. Embracing growth encourages us to seek resources to fill our voids, including incorporating lived experience, social support, and professional help.

While embracing the reality that perfection is not possible, we acknowledge that encouragement can be sought from others. Social support can come in many forms, such as offering insight to lighten blind spots, providing feedback from relatable roads, and collaboratively approaching boundary design. Teamwork in boundaries can begin with suggestions for the journey; when possible, it can encompass boundary cocreation as well. This allows all involved to assist with fortifying resourceful parameters. And since boundary design can be a challenging process, in times which general social support is insufficient, a growth mindset can motivate us to seek professional guidance (such as therapy) for our journey.

DESIGNING HEALTHY BOUNDARIES

REFLECTION

In what ways has your self-growth strengthened over time? What opportunities might you take to cultivate self-growth in the future?

_____

_____

_____

_____

_____

_____

_____

✏️ CORINNE, PARKER, SAVI, DAVE, AND RAE

Review what you have learned about Corinne (page 29), Parker (page 20), Savi (page 36), and Dave and Rae (page 40). Use the prompts below to explore their self-love strengths and opportunities for growth. For reference you can use The Seven Segments of Self-Love worksheet in the appendix on page 188. Feel free to expand this activity by completing that worksheet for each person.

Strengths

Corinne

_____

_____

_____

_____

_____

Parker

_____

_____

_____

_____

_____

Savi

_____

_____

_____

_____

_____

Dave

_____

_____

_____

_____

_____

Rae

_____

_____

_____

_____

_____

DESIGNING HEALTHY BOUNDARIES

Opportunities for Growth

Corinne

_____

_____

_____

_____

Parker

_____

_____

_____

_____

Savi

_____

_____

_____

_____

Dave

_____

_____

_____

_____

_____

Rae

_____

_____

_____

_____

· · · · · · ·

DESIGNING BOUNDARIES WITH SELF-LOVE

Now that we have a stronger sense of what self-love is all about and how it enables us to better love others, it's time to add boundaries into the mix. First of all, it's important to establish interpersonal parameters to protect yourself. This isn't because you don't care about others; in fact, it can be because you genuinely do. For example, when we're taking quality time with our loved ones, we need to establish boundaries at the workplace to protect that family time. In this sort of scenario, context, values, priorities, and people all factor in. One could argue that the time off demonstrates that we don't respect our occupational responsibilities. However, it may actually be a domino effect: tending to our needs while investing in quality time with loved ones helps us to recharge—and be more engaged, motivated, and resourceful at work. In this example, self-love in the present moment honors ourselves and our loved ones, while in the wider picture it honors everyone involved, including our colleagues.

📁 **PARKER**—To recollect what we know about Parker, see page 20.

Parker's parents separated in his first year of college. From that point forward, the established connection he'd always had between loved ones and football began to fissure as the family grew apart. In his junior year, his mother was diagnosed with early-onset Alzheimer's disease. When he went home for spring break to visit his mother for her birthday, he noticed that she had stopped taking her medications and had been skipping medical appointments. So Parker transferred to a nearby college for his senior year and took on the role of caretaker—doing his best to manage his personal obligations in between his caretaker priorities. With limited resources, he unintentionally began to neglect his well-being. And while the stress of his mother's declining health amplified his focus on her wellness, he struggled to maintain his own, especially without his former healthy diet and the vigorous exercise of football practice. Then, at his next annual physical, he learned he was pre-diabetic.

Consider what you know about Parker as you explore the following prompts:

Did Parker's boundary domains and levels change over the years? What obstacles challenged Parker's healthy boundary design? How can Parker infuse self-love into his boundaries to help himself and his mother?

_____

_____

_____

_____

_____

_____

Boundaries are commonly considered to be interpersonal guidelines. When you shift your focus to not just *consider* the role of the self but also prioritize it, it can seem a bit daunting. Self-love in boundaries requires you to look inward when social situations go awry. The purpose of this shift is to foster the recognition of yourself in the process, to strengthen your agency, and to promote your ownership when needed. It is important to note that enhancing accountability and responsibility does not need to be bundled with blame and shame. Recognizing your role in the efficacy of your boundaries by no means suggests you are at fault for all struggles you experience with them. In addition, while self-love is the founding force for designing boundaries, effective interpersonal boundaries call for energy from all parties involved. Moreover, some of the healthiest boundaries are supported by mutual love. When all parties collaborate and infuse self-love, kind, caring, and respectful boundaries tend to arise.

A self-loving method of boundary design emphasizes *you*. After all, you know the true you. When you hone your self-awareness and foster self-knowledge through the continued process of exploration, you're able to become the best expert in *you*. Note, though, that this isn't about knowing it all. Again, no one is perfect, and even the most self-aware of us can't help but have blind spots. And while blind spots arise from and affect our view at the personal level, they can permeate to interpersonal boundaries as well. And so, you can benefit from carefully permitting others to inform your boundaries. Trustworthy loved ones or professional helpers can be great resources for shining a light into your personal blind spots.

📁 **CORINNE**—To recollect what we know about Corinne, see page 29.

Corinne's husband's infidelity caused her to spiral into an emotional rollercoaster. After concluding that many people take her for granted, she decided to make a drastic change and enact boundaries. Instead of putting others first, she decided to enforce rigid boundaries across the board. Her best friend Maria noticed a shift in not only their friendship but in all Corinne's relationships, from her children to her neighbors. She also saw how unhappy Corinne was, so Maria invited Corinne for coffee. From their conversation, in which Corinne shared much more about her life than she'd shared previously, it was clear that Corinne believed others were constantly taking advantage of her. When Corinne made a few quips about Maria's lack of appreciation for their own friendship, Maria knew she needed to speak her truth. She began by sharing her genuine value for their relationship over the decades. Then she confessed how hard it can be to support Corinne, since she often keeps things to herself, rarely shares what she desires, and readily jumps to fulfill everyone else's needs. From hearing this well-intentioned message from Maria, Corinne realized that perhaps she's been a people-pleaser.

The above scenario includes the overstepping of interpersonal boundaries, especially that of Corinne and her husband. However, Corinne may have also overlooked the value of designing and honoring her own personal parameters. Neglecting this foundational layer may have made it easier for others to dismiss her needs.

While self-love may be empowering, that doesn't mean you'll have full control. Just as perfection is an illusion, so is absolute control in this framework. Emergencies like dealing with an illness or an unexpected accident will challenge established boundaries—as can other people and social systems. Further, our natural blind spots can keep us from realizing that factors that appear to be within our control are actually fluid. What appears to suit you perfectly today will not always fit perfectly in the future. When you adopt this truth, you can better invest your energy. At the least, you can make a distinction between what is within your realm of management and what is beyond your control—and hence must be surrendered.

When you design boundaries with self-love, many times this elicits opportunities for you to better love yourself, love others, and allow others to love you in return. However, remember that this doesn't necessarily mean you have to love everyone you set boundaries with, or that you'll love every aspect of the boundary-design process. Not all boundaries will elicit love. Peripheral boundaries, such as those you hold generally with people you don't know, certainly don't require the intimacy of love in the process. However, since all boundaries are technically personal boundaries, you have the opportunity to establish each parameter by loving yourself.

Again, designing healthy boundaries can be a challenging process. It's understandable if you feel frustrated, disappointed, and angry at times—which can make it harder to enjoy the process. However, even in these moments, remember that taking breaks, acknowledging your troubles, asking for help, enduring despite the challenge, and continuing on are all ways to show yourself love when you need it the most.

CHAPTER 5

BOUNDARY DOMAINS: WHO ARE YOU?

Self-love serves as a catalyst for establishing purposeful parameters. You can begin to set a foundation of self-love by asking four core questions: Who are you? What do you believe? How do you find balance? Where do you have the opportunity to grow? This chapter begins with the first question, while the next three chapters cover the remaining questions. You'll later revisit these activities at a later phase of the process. See also the Boundary Domains worksheet on page 189 in the appendix.

WHO ARE YOU?

We are all unique. Each of us is a special combination of traits, preferences, abilities, beliefs, interests, desires, and connections. These parts coalesce to form our overall identity.

✎ PIECES OF IDENTITY

The following questions may help to start off your self-exploration:

What do you know about your lineage?

_____

_____

Whom do you spend the most time with?

_____

_____

What skills do you have now that you didn't have when you were younger?

_____

_____

What does a typical day look like in your world?

_____

_____

What do your loved ones believe about you?

_____

_____

What are a few things that you find fascinating?

_____

_____

What do you believe about life?

_____

_____

What are some of your favorite things about yourself?

_____

_____

If you could be anywhere in the world right now, where would that be?

_____

_____

If you could relive any memory, which would you choose?

_____

_____

If you could change three things about your life, what would they be?

_____

_____

· · · · · · ·

Small segments coalesce to form your overall identity. Examples include traits such as your appearance, characteristics such as your personality type, skills such as your field of work, or preferences such as how you like to spend your time off. These segments can provide hints about where you may benefit from boundaries. The pieces that pack a lot of power often inform your core self and tend to highlight the areas where protection may be the most warranted. For example, those who describe themselves as family people may benefit from boundaries that support quality relationships and quality personal time. The following activity can help you identify which pieces of your identify could benefit from healthy boundaries.

REFLECTION

By this point you have likely considered where you could benefit from establishing boundaries. Use the space below to list the areas that come up for you.

_____

_____

_____

_____

✎ NUANCES OF IDENTITY

Before forming boundaries or working to improve a present parameter, it can be helpful to first explore several dimensions of yourself. For example, what parts of your identity are tender? What parts are tough? What parts of your identity are hidden? What parts are on display? What parts of your identity are new? What parts are established? What parts of your identity are deep? What parts are superficial? For this activity, choose one boundary that you're currently brainstorming, gauge where this boundary falls along each of the four spectrums, and reflect on the lines to follow.

Boundary: _____

Tender–Tough: The pieces of your identity may encompass a broad range. Understanding where they lie across the following dimensions can help you to identify what you may need to design healthy boundaries around. For example, parts of your identity can be tender, while others can be tough. Knowing what areas are tender can help you to establish boundaries that offer the gentleness and care those parts warrant. These delicate pieces usually need more patience, time, and attention, especially at the personal level. On the other hand, tough pieces can serve as bold strengths. Perhaps they designate areas bolstered by strong boundary protection. That said, some areas can be unnecessarily firm, perhaps indicating areas that have been so tightly protected that they've left you disconnected from others.

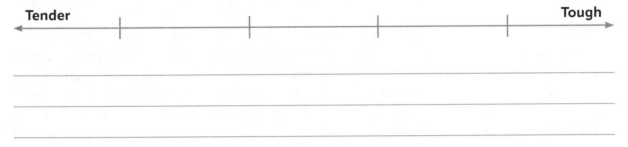

Hidden–Displayed: Parts of your identity can be hidden, while others can be apparent. And since we all have blind spots, there can be aspects of our identity that we're not cognizant of. Even when we are aware of these details, that doesn't mean we're comfortable divulging them with everyone. While there are a variety of reasons to maintain your privacy (particularly for safety), sometimes it can be complicated for others to honor our well-designed boundaries without understanding the underlying cause. Well-designed boundaries are often clear from both ends of setting and receiving. This clarity makes it easier to readily remember, reference, and put into practice.

Hidden ←———|———————|———————|———————|———→ Displayed

_____

_____

_____

New–Established: Parts of your identity can be rather new, while others can be well-established. The pieces that are new may have come to light due to recent events. Some areas that seem new may have already been in existence—but for some reason you weren't aware of them until now. Sometimes these are just blind spots; sometimes they signify a realm in which you've had some friction, such as disappointing outcomes, low confidence in your abilities, or simply your own stubbornness. Fortunately, it can be much easier to form boundaries for newer pieces since there's not a lot to undo and redo. On the other hand, facets that are long-established may be trickier to design healthy boundaries for, as the routes may be deeply ingrained.

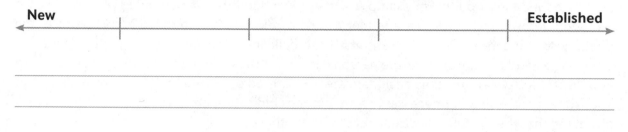

Deep–Superficial: Parts of your identity can run deep, while others can be at surface level. The pieces within the depths of our identity are often attributes of our core self, the key details that make us who we are, the aspects of our identity that resonate with our deeper meaning. Being near and dear to us, these are often areas that we would benefit from firm protection—from ourselves and others. On the other hand, surface-level aspects of who we are may need only limited protection. For example, consider that two friends plan to meet for lunch. For one of them, who has no dietary concerns, the details of menu, location, and availability may not mean much—whereas for the other, who has diabetes and is vegan, those details are essential.

· · · · · · ·

✏️ IDENTITY ROLES

Use the space provided to brainstorm about your roles, such as partner, parent, child, sibling, colleague, friend, neighbor, etc. Consider these questions: What are some of the roles that you hold? What are some of the qualities of each role? Which roles are the most important to you?

Example:

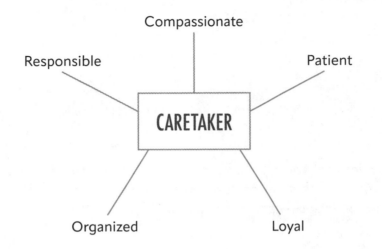

Consider the different contexts that commonly apply in your life, such as the different environments you've found yourself in within the last month or so (e.g., home, office, store, park, neighbor's BBQ, airport, etc.). Place those examples in the box below.

Select one of the roles that you explored (page 69) and three contexts you listed in the box above. How does your role shift per context? What remains the same? What showed up as a prominent trend? What do you recognize could be an opportunity for growth?

_____

_____

_____

_____

_____

_____

_____

· · · · · · ·

CHAPTER 6

BOUNDARY DOMAINS: WHAT DO YOU BELIEVE?

Tuning in to your thoughts and beliefs gives you a window to the world around you as well as the world within you. Further, you can see how your inner world and the environment/experiences affect one another—or, at minimum, how you perceive them to affect one another. For example, consider your views about how you want to spend your days. If you believe that life is best spent with your loved ones, then that could inform the importance of creating boundaries to protect that connecting time. Contemplating your thoughts and beliefs can help you identify where boundaries are needed in your life, why they are needed in those areas, how to support those boundaries, and what may stand in the way of your healthy boundary-design journey. As we explore these important thoughts, we will start from the outside in.

REFLECTION

Healthy boundaries are designed with a purpose. To highlight where you could utilize boundaries to improve your well-being it can be helpful to consider your why. *You have already made it this far: Why? What is the purpose of investing the time and energy into this process?*

OTHERS' BELIEFS

Beliefs are not consistent across people. We hold different perspectives about ourselves and others, the world, what matters most in the world, and what we need to do to protect these areas of importance. When others around us have thoughts that differ from our own, friction may arise. Through communication and compromise, sometimes mutual understanding and respect can be achieved. However, it is not necessarily our responsibility to reduce the tension, especially in terms of ensuring others' perspectives conform to our own and vice versa. Often-times our energy can be better invested by acknowledging the friction and utilizing the identified discrepancy to inform our boundary design.

✎ TRICKLING THOUGHTS

Think of a time when you experienced friction due to you and someone else having opposing beliefs. In the box on the left, explore your beliefs from that occasion. In the box on the right, describe how you perceive the other's beliefs.

Situation: _____

My Beliefs	How I Perceived Other's Beliefs

Next, zoom out to explore this conflict from a wider perspective.

What boundaries could have been helpful in this situation?

_____

_____

_____

_____

_____

Our thoughts and beliefs are often influenced by the groups in which we belong, regardless of whether or not we want to absorb their messages. Thoughts others have about us also tend to influence our thoughts about ourselves over time, whether or not our surrounding systems are healthy. This potential is heightened when we are young, struggling with self-esteem, in a vulnerable position, and/or are close to or inspired by the people sharing their opinions and beliefs. Generally speaking, this is not problematic when the messages are neutral or positive. But when the messages are toxic or phony we may benefit from establishing boundaries from them.

In the space below, explore the groups in which you belong, some common beliefs in those groups, and how those beliefs influence your beliefs. You may find it helpful to look back to the Nuances of Identity activity (page 66) for inspiration.

When you explore how you're influenced by the groups in which you belong, inspiration for boundary design may begin to surface. Rereading what you've explored above, place a check mark near the beliefs that you feel good about, the ones where you're satisfied with the influence they have on you. Next, place an asterisk near the examples you're not satisfied with. Now, look at what you've identified. You may want to design boundaries that continue to foster the connections you appreciate, the ones noted with a check mark. For the ones noted with an asterisk, you'd be wise to create boundaries to separate those unsatisfactory thoughts from permeating your own.

• • • • • • •

VALUES

A shortcut to uncovering where boundaries would be beneficial in your life would be to ask yourself what means the most to you. Your values serve as the code to your identity. The beliefs you hold inform how you view yourself, how you perceive others, how you see the world, and how you choose to exist within the world. What you find most meaningful provides a compass for you to navigate boundaries. When you are cognizant of your deeper meaning, you can design intentional boundaries and live a purposeful life. When you connect to your values, you practice self-love. Building boundaries that support your value-alignment is an act of self-respect. This practice can pave a path for others to offer you respect by honoring the boundaries that they observe you forming with intentionality, connecting to with dedication, and asserting with confidence.

✎ EXPLORING YOUR VALUE CODE

The chart below lists a variety of common values. You may find yourself drawn to some and repelled by others—to varying degrees. Identifying which values you feel the most strongly about can help you to better understand yourself, define your core values, and design healthy boundaries.

Use the value key to label each value in the chart below.

VALUE KEY

---	--	-	0	+	++	+++
Extremely Unimportant	Very Unimportant	Somewhat Unimportant	Neutral	Somewhat Important	Very Important	Extremely Important

VALUE CHART

Achievement	Collaboration	Faith
Altruism	Comfort	Fame
Ambition	Communication	Flexibility
Awareness	Cooperation	Freedom
Beauty	Connection	Fun
Certainty	Consistency	Generosity
Charity	Courage	Growth
Chastity	Creativity	Happiness
Cleanliness	Dedication	Harmony

Health

Honesty

Humility

Humor

Kindness

Learning

Logic

Love

Loyalty

Neutrality

Originality

Patience

Patriotism

Peace

Politeness

Practicality

Productivity

Prosperity

Quality

Recreation

Reflection

Respect

Responsibility

Restraint

Sacrifice

Science

Security

Selflessness

Sincerity

Solitude

Spirituality

Stability

Structure

Traditionalism

Versatility

Wealth

Additional values:

_____

_____

_____

_____

_____

_____

_____

_____

_____

_____

_____

_____

After you have labeled each value above, place them into their corresponding sections below.

--	
-	
0	

+	
+	
+++	

✎ REFINING YOUR RANKING

As you look at your value chart, what do you notice? The following activities may help you further assess the depth of your values, including whether you've intuitively placed your values in their rightful section or if you should move a few.

As you contemplate the spot where you placed each value, notice what comes up for you. You may experience a flash of memories related to a particular value. If so, tune in to the memory and consider how boundaries might apply to it.
The value chart lists *common* values. If you added values to the list, you likely have strong beliefs about that value. Explore the meaning behind each value you added.
Your values are often influenced by the groups in which you belong, such as the nation you're a citizen of or the lineage you're a part of. For each positive value, explore which of your groups support that value. Ideally our values mesh nicely with those of the groups we're a part of, but they don't always. It's important to notice both the similarities and the incongruities.
Take a piece of paper and cut it into rectangular tiles. Write one of your values in each tile. Mix them up randomly. Then, organize them according to the degree to which you value each.
Choose two values at random. How do they compare? Is one more meaningful to you than the other? Continue comparing different pairs of values.
Think about how you spent the last month. How closely do your higher-ranked values align with last month's activities? How closely do they align with how you spend most of your time? Are any of the values that don't resonate for you a part of your everyday life? If so, explore why. Can you think of a time in your life when your higher-ranked values most aligned with your daily life?

✎ DECODING YOUR VALUES

Understanding where your values land on the spectrum can be helpful in designing healthy boundaries. Each domain can convey important considerations for creating, asserting, and healing in the boundary process. Let's take a moment to consider the values that you categorized as being unimportant to you. Sometimes negative beliefs about particular values derive from our having had poor encounters with them, and oftentimes poor boundaries are implicated in that. Say you were raised in a highly structured environment. If it caused you to feel restricted and uncomfortable, you may view structure poorly and avoid forming boundaries that support structure—even though you could benefit from having some degree of structure in your life. If you can identify any such unpleasant experiences, that may be a sign that healing is warranted in that area. You'll also want to consider developing boundaries in relation to the values to which you assigned negative scores. It's important to have a clear sense of what you view positively and what you view negatively—especially if there are more negative values in your life than positive. Healthy boundaries can protect you from wasting energy on that which you don't value.

In the space below, explore if any of the concepts you rated negatively were impacted by an experience that warrants healthier boundaries.

_____

_____

_____

_____

_____

Note that your having assigned some values as neutral or negative doesn't necessarily signal danger. Take, for example, two military veterans who served together. Based on their individual experiences, one may rate patriotism negatively while the other rates it positively. Neither is right or wrong. But the friction between their belief systems could warrant healthy boundaries, especially regarding respect and communication. Additionally, consider how a vet who rates patriotism negatively may have previously felt the opposite—such as when they first enlisted. As noted before, our views about our experiences likely shift over time. When we experience a shift in our values, we may benefit from reassessing our boundaries to assure they are still protecting what matters most to us, at both the personal and interpersonal levels.

REFLECTION

Have you experienced a time when a value shift—your own or someone else's—caused confusion that would have benefited from a healthy boundary?

_____

_____

_____

_____

Let's now consider the values you positioned in the middle of your spectrum—the neutral ones that are simply unimportant to you without being negative per se. For some, you might never have had strong feelings about them either way. For others, perhaps the passage of time has softened a previous negative assessment into a neutral one. We'll want to take a moment to consider the concepts in this neutral domain, since a lack of clarity can hinder healthy boundary design.

REFLECTION

Consider the values that you rated as being neutral to you. Can you explore why each is neutral to you? If for any you're unsure of why you feel neutral, explore associations to help shed light on your reasoning. What does each of these values mean to you? What does each remind you of? What is your history with each value?

_____

_____

_____

_____

_____

The concepts in your highest-ranked tier emphasize areas in which you could benefit from boundaries in order to keep yourself aligned with what matters most to you. Your core values are usually the three to five values you assigned this high ranking. If you have more than five in this section, see if a second assessment would help you to isolate the values that are truly the most important to you. This is because you'd be wise to create boundaries to protect your core values.

My Core Values

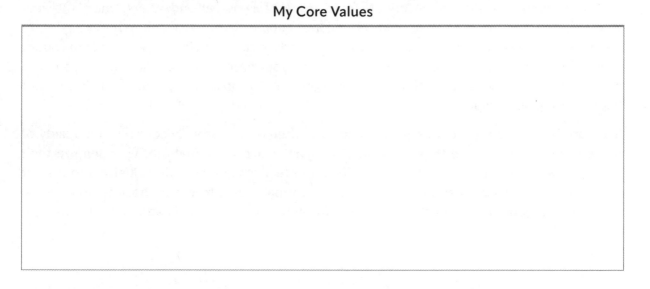

REFLECTION

Now, reflect on how your core values can help you to design healthy boundaries.

_____

_____

_____

_____

_____

_____

_____

_____

_____

_____

BELIEFS ABOUT YOURSELF

The beliefs you hold about yourself inform your boundaries. Put simply, if you hold yourself in poor regard, you're less likely to design healthy boundaries for yourself—much less maintain them or effectively assert them. On the other hand, when you recognize your intrinsic worth, you can honor it by forming boundaries to foster respect for yourself and others. One of the ways your beliefs about yourself affect your boundaries concerns your self-talk. When you do not value yourself, this will permeate through your inner dialogue. Even if you have thoughts about setting boundaries, critical self-talk can discourage your process. In contrast, when you have healthy thoughts about yourself, you can be intentional, motivated, and resilient throughout the boundary-setting process.

Because this self-talk exists within our minds, we often do not stop to consider the quality of these thoughts. And since these thoughts are "just" our own, sometimes we minimize their power. However, our self-talk doesn't just affect our feelings and behaviors; it also informs our communication and connection with others. Given that intent to design healthy boundaries, this is a great juncture at which to begin confronting poor self-beliefs and cultivate stronger ones.

✎ SOME BELIEFS ABOUT YOURSELF

In the space below, explore your beliefs about yourself. Write a belief about yourself in each of the following rectangles. (For example, "I am loving," "I am resourceful," "I am forgiving," etc.) Then, use the branched lines to explore the thoughts that come to mind when you contemplate each belief. Add more rectangles as needed.

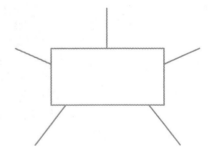 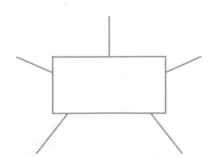

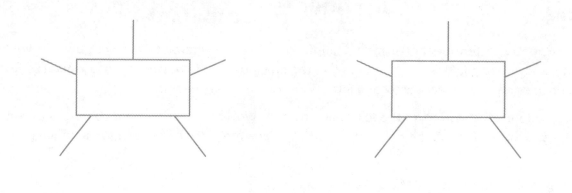

. . . .

As you explore your beliefs, you may find some are harder to contemplate than others. Since perfection is not an objective of the healthy boundary-design process, try to utilize this as a chance to practice reframing your self-talk. For example, let's say you believe you're indecisive. What words might you write around your "indecisive" circle? What are more positive spins you could put on this self-assessment? Perhaps "I am easy-going," "I value a variety of perspectives," and "I have an opportunity to grow in making decisions." Note that these reframes don't whitewash your experience, they just offer paths toward a more positive outlook. (Also, if it's not already included in your beliefs, now is a good time to add "I am worthy of healthy boundaries"—and to embrace the enhanced self-esteem that follows as you continue your journey.)

MANTRAS AND BOUNDARY DESIGN

Encouraging self-thoughts are helpful in the boundary-design process. They help you to highlight your strengths and motivate you to grow through your challenges. They serve as quick, power-packed reminders throughout the cycle of creation, assertion, and healing. One way to support your beliefs about yourself and encourage healthy boundaries is by incorporating mantras.

A mantra—originally from the Sanskrit for "sacred speech"—is a select set of purposeful words you combine to hone your intention and affirm your intrinsic worth. When you carefully curate your selection, you artfully offer yourself a special resource to improve your focus, determination, and resilience. The process of forming a mantra is the first part of this unique gift from you to you. As you establish the ritual of routinely reciting your mantra, each time you speak it you offer yourself the present of being present in your power.

The options for repeating your mantra range from quiet and personal to creative and candid, such as inspiration for a painting, shirt, or tattoo. Recitation of your mantra can be particularly useful at all points in the boundary-design process—as well as, in fact, any time.

✎ CREATING BOUNDARY-DESIGN MANTRAS

When creating intentional mantras it's helpful to reflect on where you are now, how far you've come, and where you'd like to go—as well as the gracious gaps in between those junctures. Start by considering your history with, and intentions for, boundary design.

Next, explore your answers to the following prompts. We'll be revisiting what you explore here in a later section, so it might be helpful to write on a separate piece of paper or on a device of your choosing.

As you look at the past and the present:

- What had you hoped would change?
- What has changed?
- What may have fostered those changes?
- What do you wish had stayed the same?
- What has stayed the same?
- What may have maintained this stability?

Use the reflections above to inform your intentional responses below. As you look at the present and the future:

- How can you foster stability going forward?
- What can you do to cultivate strength going forward?
- How can you infuse hope going forward?
- What can you do to encourage growth?
- How can you build support for the days to come?

Next, consider words that have affected you positively. Maybe words that have floated across your own mind, something you heard, or something said to you by someone you value. Perhaps quotes from a person you admire, lyrics from a song you enjoy, or words from a book you love. In the space below, brainstorm the phrases that empower you.

By now you've had the opportunity to think about what you'll need for the boundary-design process as well as words that have inspired you to date. Now, let's merge these two reflections in tailoring your mantras. To start you off I'll share a few examples:

Life is beautiful

Progress over perfection

I am capable of growth

I am enough

Healthy mind, healthy relationships

My boundaries matter

· · · · · · ·

CHAPTER 7

BOUNDARY DOMAINS: HOW DO YOU FIND BALANCE?

Balance offers a path of wellness. When key areas of life are stable, we're able to experience a sense of peace. Our minds become calm and moments occur with ease. We may find ourselves fortunate to arrive to a sense of harmony across our values, feelings, choices, and actions. Balance can look different from person to person, and the formula can shift for one person over time. Additionally, some phases in our lives may challenge our footing more than others. However, even in times when equilibrium feels disrupted, or seems impossible, we can stabilize our well-being just by offering ourselves solid footing.

Though the ability to acquire balance starts from within, it can be affected by the world around you. This includes the environments you find yourself in, the relationships you're connected to, and the systems you're a part of. With this in mind, a key aspect of boundary design is to understand what balance looks like in your life and what boundaries you could benefit from forming in order to evoke, maintain, and protect your well-being.

REFLECTION

In order to acquire balance, first we need to define "wellness" for ourselves. What does it mean to you? What key words come to mind? What does it look like when you are well? What is present to make this possible? What is notably absent?

_____

_____

_____

_____

_____

HOW DO YOU FIND BALANCE?

Oftentimes we reduce wellness to a simple, even singular view. Due to society's emphasis on physical health, when we consider wellness, aspects of physiological well-being commonly come to mind (e.g., nutrition, exercise). While these aspects are certainly important, they are likely not all-encompassing. A comprehensive view of wellness is useful for gaining a wider, and more accurate, perception of what your well-being entails.

✎ COMMON WELLNESS DOMAINS

To follow is a list of common wellness domains. Circle the ones that are important to you. Perhaps add a star next to the domains that are essential to your well-being. If there are aspects of your wellness that are not represented by the following terms, add your own to the list.

Cultural	Personal	_____
Digital	Physical	_____
Educational	Relational	_____
Emotional	Sexual	_____
Environmental	Social	_____
Familial	Spiritual	_____
Financial	_____	_____
Interpersonal	_____	_____
Mental	_____	_____
Nutritional	_____	
Occupational		

· · · · · · ·

REFLECTION

Next, explore what wellness can mean for you. Here are a few prompts to help you:

What lesson(s) have you learned about your health? Growing up, what areas of wellness were you encouraged to foster? Do you feel energized after seeing loved ones, spending time alone, or both? When you are sick, what do you turn to? Think of a happy memory. What contributed to that moment? When you imagine yourself in one year, what area(s) would you like to grow in? In what areas of your life have you had thoughts about adding boundaries? Think of someone who inspires you. What aspects of wellness do they foster?

✎ YOUR WELLNESS FORMULA

Now that you've reflected on what dimensions of wellness are important to you, refine these categories to help you understand your model of wellness. Revisit the terms you singled out in the list of common wellness domains (page 85). Notice which words seem similar. Should some be combined? Or are they related yet distinct? Aim to narrow them down to five to eight domains and note them in the space below.

Now that you know your essential wellness domains, reflect on the following for each:

What makes this category important to you?

_____

_____

What is your history in this area?

_____

_____

How does this area foster your well-being?

_____

_____

Think of the time when this area was functioning most optimally. What may have attributed to that?

_____

_____

Think of a time when this area was functioning least optimally. What may have attributed to that?

_____

_____

What are signs that this domain is helping you thrive?

_____

_____

What are signs that this domain is keeping you from thriving?

_____

_____

Generally speaking, how much of this area is needed in order for you to be well? What is your bare minimum? Is there such a thing as too much of this area?

_____

_____

_____

· · · · · · ·

Taking a snapshot of your wellness formula can help you to understand where you may benefit from creating intentional boundaries. It's particularly helpful to reflect on where your wellness once was, where it is now, and where you wish it to be. As you do so keep in mind that, while some practices can contribute to more than one domain at a time, it's unrealistic for all areas to be consistently at their pinnacle. For example, while engaging in this workbook can cultivate all abovementioned domains of wellness in some form, nevertheless, all of your wellness domains will not necessarily be completely fulfilled each time you work on this book.

A visual depiction of your wellness formula can help you to notice where healthy boundaries are warranted. Use the upcoming activity to illustrate what your wellness has looked like, what it appears to be today, and what it may look like for the future. While that might sound daunting, it doesn't have to be. You can gauge your wellness by looking at a given day, week, or month. For example, how much energy did you invest in each dimension last week? What would you want to invest next week?

When considering your past, current, and future wellness domains, you may find it helpful to infuse a blend of realism and optimism as you assess your hopeful intentions. For example, if you genuinely have the grand goal of becoming a billionaire, your financial domain may require a substantial investment—and in order to make that possible, it's likely that other dimensions of your well-being would have to be lowered markedly to enable this goal.

✎ EXPLORING YOUR WELLNESS FORMULA

Using the empty graph on the following page, write in your wellness domains underneath the bottom horizontal line. Based on the hour measurements on the left, for each domain, you'll next create vertical bars indicating the amount of energy (a) that you've spent in the past and (b) that you're currently spending. Later you'll create a third column indicating what you commit to spending in the future. (See the Example Wellness-Domain Investment Bar Graph for reference.)

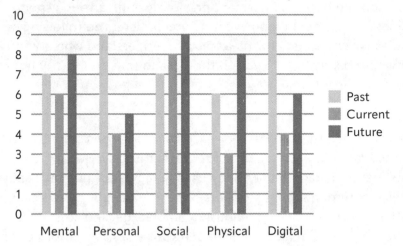

Example Wellness-Domain Investment Bar Graph

✎ CLARIFYING YOUR WELLNESS FORMULA

After you've indicated the hour commitment previously and currently spent on each domain, look at your wellness-investment graph; what do you notice? The following sections may help you to further assess your wellness formula to better understand where you can benefit from designing healthy boundaries to help you to thrive—and thus how many hours per domain to commit to spending in the future.

SURVIVAL MODE

Take a glance at your wellness domains. For each category, consider what would be the bare minimum you would need in each area in order to not just survive but thrive. These aspects are clues for personal boundaries, since they usually represent nonnegotiables. Let's say for example that you've determined that six hours of quality sleep is a physical necessity for you. You've learned this because you've previously gambled getting less sleep—in quality and/or quantity—and recognize that sleep deprivation causes a cascade of concerns across your wellness dimensions. When boundaries are infused with self-love, bringing this humble acknowledgment to your awareness encourages you to establish parameters that support this core need in order to foster your overall wellness. Therefore, you need to set a nonnegotiable boundary about getting at least six hours of quality sleep per night. Now, let's say that a friend is going through a rough patch. In fact, let's make that friend Corinne, who we've met before. You offer support and compassion by spending time talking with her. If Corinne calls you at midnight after she's had a particularly distressing day, you may be tempted to bend your sleep boundary so as to be a loving friend. But if she gets into the habit of calling late and you don't assert your boundary, ultimately both of you will struggle—when your wellness becomes depleted, you won't be able to offer her the genuine kindness you wish to.

_____

_____

_____

_____

_____

PERSONAL PREFERENCE

Another way to assess how much time to invest in your different wellness domains is to consider: do any strike you as being essential to _you_? These aren't simply necessary for your survival, but key to your identity—details specific to who you are and what matters most to you. To find inspiration for these personal elements you may find it helpful to glance back at your identity components and core values. Since these aspects aren't necessities of survival we all too readily minimize them to make special accommodations for those we care about. Out of fear of burdening others with a big ask, we may self-sacrifice by not sharing these boundaries. However, in doing so we deplete our own wellness, and our ability to care for others, too. Which domains do you notice are integral to who you are?

LEARNED LESSONS

Now we want to zero in on how much energy to commit to each wellness domain for the upcoming year. You can see what your past commitment was and what you're currently investing. Where do you want to be one year from now? What will you need to do differently in order to make that happen? Think back on any aspects of your life that hinder your ability to thrive. What have you learned that can be used to cultivate continued wellness? For example, what obstacles stood in your way? How can those be managed? What has supported your wellness journey? How can you continue that path? Reflecting on your wellness history can help you make informed choices about how to design your boundaries.

IDENTIFYING YOUR FUTURE ENERGY INVESTMENT

Now, based on what you've concluded from reviewing this section, return to your bar graph to add your projections of how much energy you would like to invest in each domain in the upcoming year.

· · · · · · ·

📁 **MARIA**

Maria deeply empathizes with Corinne in struggling with her husband's infidelity, so she's decided to be there for her friend. Unfortunately, since Corinne struggles with boundaries, she doesn't think twice about calling Maria whenever she's feeling overwhelmed—sometimes late at night. Maria, on the other hand, has been working hard to design healthy boundaries, and she's long known that she needs a minimum of six hours of quality sleep per night. The first time Corinne called Maria late, Maria knew that missing her ideal bedtime one night wouldn't devastate her wellness. Moreover, Maria values connection, and in this incident the amount of sleep does not hold a candle to the enhanced connection she feels in helping Corinne. But, since Maria knows that Corinne doesn't really understand boundaries, she senses she'll need to assert her bedtime boundary before long.

GOOD INTENTIONS

Now that you've committed to enhancing your wellness, you'll want to create boundaries that support your wellness intentions. Consider the gaps between your present and projected wellness and offer yourself a realistic reflection of what is required to close that gap. Remember that resources are finite, so an increase in one area will require a reduction in another.

You've already indicated the bare minimum of time you plan to dedicate to each area (see your notes on what your Survival Mode needs would be on page 90). Next, you might want to consider what incremental steps will be necessary to surpass these minimums and align with your intentions in each domain. For example, what does it take to ensure you get consecutive nights of sufficient, quality rest? For many, the precursors would include reducing light exposure, disconnecting from technology, and calming our bodies. From there, we can establish boundaries to protect that routine, such as being home, eating dinner, and tending to our evening tasks by a certain time.

 INTENTIONS TOWARD WELLNESS

Describe how you intend to align with your wellness.

_____

_____

_____

· · · · · · ·

SELF-CARE

It's important for us to have boundaries to encourage and protect self-care. This includes both personal parameters that motivate us to engage in self-care and interpersonal parameters that allow us to effectively practice self-care (see Self-Care on page 50). When we aren't well, we're less likely to have the energy to put toward our boundaries. If we regularly neglect our self-care, we're setting ourselves up for burnout. Over time, the gap between our need for self-care and our ability to invest in it widens. As this space expands, closing it again can seem more and more implausible, causing us to feel disheartened and ultimately disempowered. But we can prevent this hurdle and foster wellness by, first, strategizing a self-care plan; and, second, forming boundaries to ensure we have what we need to maintain our self-care.

✎ SELF-CARE STRATEGIES

A self-care kit can help you to access your strategies in times of need. Start by exploring your self-care strategies and their purposes below. You may be inspired to create a kit with tangible items from this lis; however, as long as this list is accessible, that is not required. Your wellness formula can be a helpful resource in this process as your self-care skills should stem from your domains. Since contexts shift, you will benefit from a diverse set of options in each area. You may find it helpful to include the most variety in the domains that are of priority to you.

SUGGESTED SELF-CARE STRATEGIES

Include at least one item that fits the following categories for each of your wellness domains. After each category, jot down some ideas of what to include in your plan.

ROUTINE: If you hope to foster wellness, you may find it helpful to create a habit of self-care. When you make these healing tasks a part of your everyday life, you establish a flow. Over time, you develop a rhythm, and investing in these strategies gets easier. A good place to start with routine self-care is with the foundational elements of your well-being. As you already know, sleep, hydration, nutrition, and movement are important needs for all of us. So, you can benefit from setting boundaries in place to protect these essentials on a consistent basis.

_____

_____

QUICK: Self-care may be needed when you find yourself pressed for time. Fortunately, you have the ability to tend to yourself in a prompt, efficient—albeit likely temporary—fashion. Recognizing this ability can be an empowering way for you to acknowledge the realistic limit of time, which is beyond your control, and the ability to choose to manage in the moment, which is a form of self-love. While quick tactics serve a specific purpose, they are not substitutes for comprehensive tactics. When you pull a quick strategy from your kit, it may help to link it to an intention to bolster this skill with more investment when time permits. For example, if several people are pressuring you at the same time, in the moment your options could be deep breathing or requesting a break; you could then further heal from that later with exercise, sleep, and/or therapy.

_____

_____

FREE: Yes, some self-care is expensive—but there are many no-cost and low-cost options. Consider what is currently free to you, like taking a deep breath or going for a walk. Look around your home and consider what can help you to hone your wellness. A yoga mat? A blank notebook? Beautiful cards to send a note to a friend? A special music playlist? An aromatherapy bubble bath?

_____

_____

INTERPERSONAL: Even though self-care is what you do to meet your personal needs, it doesn't have to be in solitude. Consider how you can foster your wellness by incorporating others. You might have people in your life who are on a similar journey as yours. If you know others who are also investing in building better boundaries, you can respect your individuality while mutually supporting one another. Further, accountability partners can help you to follow through on your intentions. Moreover, you do not need to walk parallel paths in order to access support. Professional help can be an excellent resource to cultivate wellness (e.g., coach, therapist, consultant, physician).

_____

_____

EASY: Some aspects of taking care of your needs will feel easy for you, and that's a great place to start. To help you identify what comes easily to you, take a moment to acknowledge your strengths and see how far you've come. Tasks that are easy for you are particularly useful when you're low on resources, since you may be able to access a level of flow or self-love that revs your energy and helps you meet your overall wellness needs.

_____

_____

CHALLENGING: Self-care isn't always simple. The harsh reality is our needs may not be an easy feat to tackle. While they may not be enjoyable, in the wider perspective, we can acknowledge that they are critical to our well-being. Therefore, when cultivating a self-care practice it is important to be honest with yourself. Be transparent regarding what your needs are and what you need to do in order to meet them. As you read this, perhaps boundaries come to mind. They may not be a walk in the park, and they may even come with arduous effort; however, they are essential. This type of humble recognition opens the door for growth and resilience.

_____

_____

Now that you've considered what self-care could look like for you, consider what parameters you may need to foster that self-care. One aspect of that is identifying which items in your plan you'll want to schedule into your week and which items you can keep in mind for when you have a bit of spare time. If you find it helpful to organize your self-care plan into a chart, the first row is partially filled in to get you started. Or you may prefer to simply identify a self-care strategy in the left column and then fill in what boundaries you'll want to establish in order to make those possible.

	Self-Care Item	Time Details (Hours/day, etc.)	Boundary Needed to Maintain	Notes/To Do/Items to Keep On Hand
Routine	Sleep	___ hours minimum/night	• No caffeine after: _____ • Unplug by: • In bed by: • Lights out by:	• Wash bedsheets on Sunday • Keep bluelight-blocking glasses by the bedside
Routine				
Routine				
Quick				
Quick				

	Self-Care Item	Time Details (Hours/day, etc.)	Boundary Needed to Maintain	Notes/To Do/Items to Keep On Hand
Free				
Free				
Interpersonal				
Interpersonal				
Easy				

	Self-Care Item	Time Details (Hours/day, etc.)	Boundary Needed to Maintain	Notes/To Do/Items to Keep On Hand
Easy				
Challenging				
Challenging				

· · · · · · ·

DESIGNING HEALTHY BOUNDARIES

CHAPTER 8

BOUNDARY DOMAINS: WHERE DO YOU HAVE THE OPPORTUNITY TO GROW?

Though the boundary-design process can be challenging, with challenge comes the chance to grow and develop perseverance and resilience—thereby expanding our knowledge of what we're capable of. As an added bonus, all this can serve our boundary design in the future.

Rather than perceiving the boundary design journey as a sprint, recognize that genuinely committing to building healthy boundaries means that you are in for a much longer haul. In actuality, forming functional boundaries isn't even much of a marathon, as there is no finish line. Rather than being time-bound, the specifications you form might pertain to your *relationship* with time. Instead of fervently pushing forward, growth may look like the ability to slow down and observe your journey. When you shift your focus from the end of your path, you offer yourself the ability to cultivate self-love as you expand in the ongoing opportunity to grow. As you trek, you can live, learn, and thrive as you explore your inner world and the world around you. With this knowledge comes the chance to gradually hone your process and commit to the ongoing investment of creating, asserting, and healing through boundaries across your lifespan.

WHERE DO YOU HAVE OPPORTUNITIES TO GROW?

In reflecting on where we need boundaries, it helps to start with the foundational reflection of where we have room to grow. It is a self-loving practice to recognize where you have opportunities to learn, improve, and strive to be the best version of yourself. Infusing this self-loving method into the lifelong boundary-design process allows you to more easily hone your knowledge of where you are and where you wish to be. In this assessment, you can benefit from welcoming feedback, considering a variety of perspectives, and reminding yourself of who you are, what you believe in, and how you seek balance. When this reflection is habitual, you are able to offer yourself opportunities to honor your present boundaries and improve them for the future.

Many attributes and abilities encompass duality. What you may categorize as a strength may not be perceived that way to others. For example, if you tend to be goal-oriented, perhaps you may have the strengths of motivation, ambition, and determination. On the flip side, perhaps patience, pacing, flexibility, and self-kindness may be opportunities for growth. Rather than seeing any of these aspects as positive or negative, offer yourself the humble perspective that we all have areas for growth at any given time.

✎ IDENTIFYING YOUR ABILITIES AND ATTRIBUTES

Use the prompts below to explore your abilities and attributes. As you delve into where you have room for growth, you may learn helpful insights to add to the previously explored questions: Who are you? (chapter 5) and How do you find balance? (chapter 7).

Exploring Your Strengths

What strengths have been consistent in your life? Explore how your boundaries may play a role in this.

_____

_____

What strengths have you recently acquired? Explore how your boundaries may play a role in this.

_____

_____

What strengths help you in understanding where you need boundaries?

_____

_____

What strengths help you to assert boundaries?

_____

_____

What strengths help you to withstand the challenges of the boundary-design process?

_____

What is the relationship between your strengths and self-love?

_____

_____

What is the current connection between your strengths and personal boundaries?

_____

_____

What is the current connection between your strengths and interpersonal boundaries?

_____

_____

You may find it helpful to create boundaries to protect your strengths. What could those look like?

_____

_____

Exploring Your Areas for Growth

What areas of growth have been consistent in your life? Explore how your boundaries may play a role in this.

_____

_____

What growth gaps have you recently acquired? Explore how your boundaries may play a role in this.

_____

_____

How can your areas for growth help you in understanding where you need boundaries?

_____

_____

How can your areas for growth help you to assert boundaries?

_____

_____

How can your areas for growth help you to withstand the challenges of the boundary-design process?

_____

_____

What is the relationship between your growth gaps and self-love?

_____

_____

What is the current connection between your areas for growth and personal boundaries?

_____

_____

What is the current connection between your areas for growth and interpersonal boundaries?

_____

_____

You may find it helpful to create boundaries to help you cultivate the areas where you have room for growth. What might those look like?

_____

_____

· · · · · · ·

INTENTIONALITY

Connecting with your intentions helps you to stay aligned in your growth process and offers a consistent tether to your truth as you navigate your journey. Understanding the underlying intention behind the boundaries is to imagine you currently have them in place you form allows you to practice self-love as you celebrate your efforts in times of alignment, offer yourself grace in times of struggle, and respond with flexibility when unexpected obstacles veer you off course.

✏️ VISUALIZATION: INTENTIONS

One way to foster healthy boundaries is to imagine you currently have them in place. For this activity, find a quiet, comfortable space. Set a timer for five minutes. Imagine for a moment that you've already invested the effort needed to cultivate strong parameters. Close your eyes and allow yourself to visualize what life would look like if you adhered to the intention of designing healthy boundaries. When the time is up, reflect below on what you visualized.

_____

_____

_____

_____

The prompts below will help you to expand on your visualization and hone your intention of healthy boundary design.

What do you hope for?

_____

_____

_____

What makes this important to you?

_____

_____

_____

Where are you in this process?

_____

_____

_____

What steps have you taken?

_____

_____

_____

How will you prepare for the path ahead?

_____

_____

_____

What support do you need for your trek?

_____

_____

_____

What obstacles do you anticipate?

_____

_____

_____

DESIGNING HEALTHY BOUNDARIES

What may tempt you to abandon your path?

_____

_____

_____

How will you know if this intention no longer suits you?

_____

_____

_____

How can you help yourself to align with this intention over time?

_____

_____

_____

Does this image differ from the one conjured at the beginning of this book (Visualization: Imagery on page 8)? If so, how?

_____

_____

_____

· · · · · · ·

✎ CONNECTING WITH YOUR INTENTIONALITY

It can be advantageous throughout the boundary-design process for you to have a deep connection with your intentionality—but sometimes it can be difficult to stay tethered to your intention. Brainstorm methods that can help you remain aligned with your intentions over time. To follow are a few examples to get you started.

- **Visualize:** Allow yourself time to immerse in the intentionality visualization.

- **Ritualize:** Create the habit of connecting to your intention in a rhythmic form, such as reciting a daily mantra, meditating, or journaling.
- **Wear your truth:** Select something that you regularly wear (such as jewelry or a watch) to associate with your intention. Then, every time you see it, you'll be reminded of your intentionality.
- **In plain sight:** Add a visual reminder that you'll regularly see in your day-to-day life, such as a note on your fridge, a sticky note on your desk, or a sticker on your laptop.
- **Periodic reminders:** Schedule regular prompts for the year ahead to remind you of your commitment, perhaps in your calendar or on your phone.

· · · · · · ·

✎ CELEBRATING SUCCESSES

When we're working hard to design better boundaries, it's easy to focus so much on identifying the gaps we still need to fill that we forget to acknowledge the progress we've made so far. Allow yourself to celebrate your achievements in this lifelong journey; offer yourself validation for all your diligence. Each victory matters—no matter how small it may seem. In actuality, the small steps accumulate into substantial change. So don't forget to take the time to regularly recalibrate by reflecting on what you've learned and utilizing that knowledge to motivate you to continue cultivating growth. In fact, take a moment now: in the space that follows, explore and honor the growth you've already achieved.

_____

_____

_____

_____

_____

_____

· · · · · · · ·

BLIND SPOTS

We all have blind spots. Even if we hone our intention of self-awareness, there will still be details beyond our view. Accepting this universal truth can help us to develop a welcoming perspective to learning new information about ourselves and the world; remind us that boundaries can always be improved; and help us to retain the flexibility that offers greater well-being. Further, this perspective can motivate us to shine a light on our blind spots. Investing in exploring blind spots can be a supportive practice in refining boundaries to meet our needs over time.

A note of caution regarding this process of exploration: once a new area has been uncovered, it's easy to focus on filling that void rather than taking a moment to learn from it. Instead, reflect on (a) what the blind spot hid, (b) how long it remained hidden, (c) what had kept it hidden, and (d) how its existence may have affected you and your boundaries. Taking the time to consider these aspects can help you to maintain effective boundaries.

✎ UNCOVERING YOUR BLIND SPOTS

One of the ways you can improve your boundary design is by intentionally incorporating methods of seeking out the blind spots into your life. A few examples are offered below. For each, consider whether it could be a beneficial strategy for you.

Reading: Exposing yourself to a wide variety of information and sources can help you to raise awareness of things you may not have previously considered.

Taking a Workshop: Being a lifetime learner is a helpful quality in forming healthy boundaries over time. You can hone your knowledge enrolling in a workshop or class.

Exploring the World: Learning doesn't have to be formal. When you're open to paying attention to the world around you, your life can be your class. Intentionally seeking out experiences that are different from your own can help to broaden your worldview.

✎ BLIND SPOTS

Think back on the blind spots you've previously held. For each blind spot, consider what they kept you from seeing, how long they were hidden, what may have kept them hidden, and how they were uncovered.

_____

_____

_____

_____

_____

Take a moment to offer yourself a broader perspective. As you review your past blind spots, do you notice any themes? For example, did they tend to occur in a similar area of self-love or wellness? Did they become uncovered at a certain phase in your life? Did something foster your excavation?

_____

_____

_____

_____

_____

Now that you've reflected on your past blind spots, consider your boundaries. How did your blind spots affect your boundaries? Knowing what you know now, how can you utilize the concept of blind spots to inform healthy boundary design?

_____

_____

_____

_____

_____

Seeking Feedback: You can bolster your boundaries by soliciting input from others. Since we all have different perspectives, people you are close to may be able to see blind spots of yours that you can't. If you're willing to ask, these trusted individuals can offer supportive feedback to help expand your awareness.

· · · · · · · ·

STRESS

Stress is the experience of pressure that affects our equilibrium. Of course, stress is a normal part of our lives and can occur in a range of forms. In smaller doses, we may not find ourselves off-kilter. There are even forms of stress that you may welcome, since the challenge comes with an opportunity for self-love. But that doesn't lessen the fact that the pressure from distress negatively impacts our well-being, and so it's important to design healthy boundaries to better recognize and manage stress.

Some stressors derive from your own internal pressure, such as worrying about how best to organize your schedule. Many stressors derive from external pressure, such as expectations from your loved ones. Stressors also exist in the world around us—such as how members of marginalized groups experience implicit and explicit bias in their everyday lives.

REFLECTION

Sometimes the process of designing healthy boundaries can be stressful in and of itself. What do you find stressful about boundary design? Where do think these stressors come from?

_____

_____

_____

_____

· · · · · · ·

✎ STRESSORS

To follow is a list of common sources of stress that people experience. Circle all the ones that you've experienced in your life. Then put a star next to the ones that currently have the biggest impact on your wellness. In the blank spaces provided, add in any stressors not listed here that also affect your well-being.

Ableism	Moving	_____
Abuse	Passing a class	_____
Accidents	Paying bills	_____
Ageism	Racism	_____
Being on time	Relationship issues	_____
Communication problems	Sexism	_____
Discrimination	Traffic	_____
Finding a job	Workplace tension	_____
Having a child	_____	_____
Illness	_____	_____
Infertility	_____	_____
Losing a job	_____	_____
Losing a loved one	_____	_____
Making others happy	_____	_____

· · · · · · ·

✎ COPING SKILLS

While self-care is the generalized practice of tending to your needs, coping skills are the specific strategies you use to balance particular stressors and achieve balance. Therefore, self-care encompasses coping skills. To follow is a list of many kinds of coping skills that can assist in a variety of situations. Circle all the ones that you've used or that you could imagine being useful. In the blank spaces provided, add in your other coping skills; this can include how you commonly cope with the stressors on page 110, even if you consider them to be unhealthy coping skills.

1. Attend a concert
2. Attend a sporting event
3. Bake
4. Breathe deeply
5. Call a helpline
6. Call an old friend
7. Clean
8. Color
9. Cook
10. Craft
11. Create an affirmation
12. Create boundaries
13. Dance
14. De-clutter
15. Donate
16. Do something nice for someone else
17. Do Yoga
18. Draw
19. Eat a healthy meal
20. Exercise
21. Embrace silence
22. Forgive someone
23. Garden
24. Get a massage

25. Get a manicure
26. Get a pedicure
27. Give a compliment
28. Give a hug
29. Go outside
30. Groom yourself
31. Hydrate
32. Journal
33. Knit
34. Light a candle
35. Light incense
36. Listen to music
37. Listen to a podcast
38. Listen to your favorite song
39. Look at old photos
40. Look at the sky
41. Make a gratitude list
42. Make a positive playlist
43. Make a mandala
44. Make travel plans
45. Meditate
46. Meet a friend
47. Nap
48. Organize

49. Paint
50. Plan a trip
51. Play a game
52. Play a sport
53. Play an instrument
54. Play video games
55. Play with a pet
56. Practice assertiveness
57. Practice mindfulness
58. Practice safe sex
59. Pray
60. Read a book or magazine
61. Read affirmations
62. Relax
63. Rearrange furniture
64. Rest
65. Run
66. Say no to negativity
67. Set a goal
68. Sew
69. Sing
70. Smile
71. Solve a puzzle
72. Spend time in nature

73. Spend time with positive people

74. Stretch

75. Study

76. Take a bath

77. Take a break

78. Take a mental health day

79. Take pictures

80. Take a shower

81. Take a therapy session

82. Take your vitamins

83. Think positively

84. Try a DIY project

85. Try a new recipe

86. Unplug from social media

87. Use a fidget toy

88. Use essential oils

89. Use visualization

90. Volunteer

91. Walk

92. Watch funny videos

93. Watch the sunset

94. Watch your favorite movie

95. Watch your favorite show

96. Work

97. Write a letter

98. Write a poem

99. Write a song

100. Write a story

_____

_____

_____

_____

_____

_____

_____

_____

· · · · · · ·

Unfortunately, not all of us have a full array of healthy coping skills—or adaptive skills—ready when we most need them. As a result, we often default to what we've always turned to in stressful moments—and those defaults aren't necessarily good for us. In fact, many of these default coping skills are actually maladaptive—they may reduce the stressor, but ultimately they cause more harm than good. For example, let's say there is a brewing conflict in your world, such as wanting to end a relationship. Avoidance is a common coping skill. In the moment, it may seem like a fair option to deter the impending stress; however, ignoring a mounting concern that is important to you can only cause it to grow in the long run.

✎ ASSESSING YOUR COPING SKILLS

Review the coping skills that you identified in the list. Add a plus sign (+) next to the adaptive skills, and a minus sign (-) next to any maladaptive skills. If there are any that you're uncertain of or that have the potential to go either way, put an asterisk (*) next to those.

Next, start to complete the following chart. In the left column, list the stressors that have the greatest impact on your well-being. Next to each, identify the coping skills that you currently use in response. An optimal goal at this juncture would be for you to find ways to convert any maladaptive coping skills into adaptive ones. Look again at the stressors that trigger you into using maladaptive skills. Can you find adaptive skills that could potentially replace some of your maladaptive skills? Add your potential options in the third column. See if you can identify feasible adaptive skills for each stressor in your chart.

Stressor	Current Coping Skills	Potential Coping Skills	Helpful Parameters

Instead of aiming to control your exposure to stress, boundaries help you to manage what you can—and decline to engage with what you can't. Now, let's consider what parameters might be useful to employ with the stressors you've identified in your chart. For example, if alcohol is a maladaptive coping skill you use to ease your social anxiety, then you may find it helpful to choose smaller gatherings, take breaks during gatherings, or attend the event with a trusted person when possible. What would help you apply your adaptive coping skills in stressful moments? Add those details in the fourth column.

· · · · · · ·

Additionally, in order to utilize coping skills, we have to be cognizant of stressors as they arrive in order to promptly act on our boundaries. When you first direct your attention to noticing stressors you may find yourself catching them in retrospect. However, as you pay more attention you can recognize your patterns and rhythms, and form boundaries to support your balance. For example, if you identify a trigger, you may then be able to set parameters before, during, and after exposure to that trigger.

I hope that you will revisit this coping skills chart many times during your journey. It can help you to be mindful of your choices and personal parameters when attempting to foster wellness in your life.

✎ PROTECTING YOURSELF FROM TOXIC THOUGHTS

It's an unfortunate reality that we can be plagued by toxic thoughts; worse still, we're so accustomed to that constant voice that its influence can wreak havoc without our even recognizing it. Fortunately, we have the potential to improve the quality of our thoughts. We can do this by striving to be intentional of our inner dialogue.

Pay attention to your thoughts for the next day. What do you notice?

_____

_____

_____

_____

_____

_____

_____

_____

IMPROVING YOUR SELF-TALK

When your inner dialogue consistently includes more critical than kind language, you may suffer a variety of consequences. For one, since designing boundaries is an act of kindness, you may not even get to invest in the process if your self-talk stifles your efforts. Two, even if you do manage to form them, you may not be able to effectively assert them. Instead, you may become distracted by unhelpful thoughts such as, "I'm never effective at setting boundaries," "There's no point in setting boundaries because nothing will change," and "This boundary is definitely going to ruin my relationship." Three, even if you do assert your boundaries, you may not always notice when they're pushed. And while you may have the intention to protect your boundaries, if you're often unkind to yourself it can be tricky to catch and hold others accountable for *their* lack of kindness. If others' unkind words are similar to your own, the familiarity may keep you from recognizing their disrespect.

✎ CHECK YOUR TOXICITY

One way you may have the opportunity to grow is by protecting yourself from your own toxic thoughts and their respective harmful consequences. Building on the "Protecting Yourself from Toxic Thoughts" reflection you completed on page 114, assess the level of toxicity in your thoughts. The following prompts may help you to detect noxious elements in your self-talk—and to form boundaries to protect yourself from them. For each thought, explore each of the questions to help inform your boundary design. If your response does not clearly fit "yes" or "no," complete these follow-up reflections.

Question	If YES...	If NO...
Is this thought kind?	What elements make this kind?	Can you rephrase with kindness in mind?
Is this thought accurate?	What facts do you have to support this thought?	What distraction(s) caused you to treat this thought as truth?
Is this thought aligned with who you are?	What elements of this statement are consistent with your identity?	What elements of your identity would you like to include in changing this thought?

Question	If YES...	If NO...
Is this thought similar to how someone has spoken to you?	By whom? When? What were those words?	How would someone you love respond to hearing this thought? What would their rephrase sound like?
Is this thought similar to how you would speak to someone else?	How have those similar statements been received?	What keeps you from speaking to someone else this way?
Is this thought healthy?	How do you know?	What would you like to change?
Would you like to create a personal boundary to keep yourself aware of thoughts like this?	What makes this important? How will you maintain this boundary?	What makes this thought safe to receive?

. . . .

✎ INCREASING CONGRUENCE AND ALIGNMENT

Designing healthy boundaries pertains not just to what we believe, but to what we believe matters most. In the Decoding Your Values exercise in chapter 6 (page 77) you illuminated your core values. You can cultivate harmony by being mindful of your core values. When your values align with your day-to-day thoughts, feelings, and behaviors, you're better able to find a sense of peace. Whereas when there is an imbalance between these areas it can cause a sense of disequilibrium. Many of us can benefit from boundaries that help us maintain a connection with your core values so that we can align them with our thoughts, feelings, and behaviors.

Add your core values to the chart below (see the My Core Values box on page 79). Add examples of thoughts, feelings, and behaviors that are both aligned and misaligned with each value. The idea is to help you identify signs of congruence versus incongruence.

		Core Values				
Aligned	Thoughts					
	Feelings					
	Behaviors					
Misaligned	Thoughts					
	Feelings					
	Behaviors					

What could help you to recognize when you're misaligned with your values? For example, perhaps you recognize that when you're misaligned you are more critical, irritable, and impulsive.

_____

_____

_____

_____

What could help you to recognize when you're aligned with your values? Perhaps you recognize that when you're aligned you have kinder thoughts, feel at peace, and are less reactive. How might you align with your values more often?

_____

_____

_____

_____

_____

_____

· · · · · · ·

INTERPERSONAL INFLUENCES

Even though others' thoughts are their own, they have the potential to permeate into our own minds. There are a variety of reasons we can be susceptible to absorbing the thoughts of others. One is proximity: if you see a particular officemate every day in person, you may be more likely to be influenced by their thoughts than if you worked remotely. Another is importance in our lives; we're more likely to be affected by the thoughts of those we care about. Or, if there is a power differential; it's easy to be influenced by the thoughts of those who hold more power than we do. Also, peer pressure and "group think" can pressure us to conform our thoughts. As such, we can often benefit from boundaries designed to detect toxicity from others.

The influence of others' thoughts can be helpful. Considering the examples offered, an optimistic colleague can contribute to a positive work environment, an artistic roommate may be resourceful in sharing ideas to style your space, an esteemed professor may offer nuanced notions that you can't Google, and a supportive community can lift you up in challenging times. One area you may have room for growth is in forming well-designed boundaries that are not so rigid that they block these helpful sources.

✎ INTERPERSONAL INFLUENCES

Revisit the identity roles that you explored in chapter 5 (page 69). For each role, consider all the people you encounter who may influence your thoughts. You can also consider a broader perspective and reflect on how the values of the social systems of your respective roles may influence you. Using the spectrum below of unhealthy-to-healthy influence, make note of where each person/social system might go.

Unhealthy   **Healthy**

Next, take a look at the entries you added to the unhealthy end of the spectrum. What do you notice?

_____

_____

_____

Now, take in the entries on the healthy end of the spectrum. What do you notice?

_____

_____

_____

Does someone around you believe your boundaries are unimportant? That may be an example of someone who belongs on the "unhealthy" end of the spectrum.

_____

_____

_____

Has someone around you shown genuine support of your boundary-design process? That may be an example of someone who belongs on the "healthy" end of the spectrum.

_____

_____

_____

As you reflect, do any specific statements come to mind? Consider in turn the comments regularly made by each of the people you added to the spectrum. Add their typical comments to the left column of the table to follow. Then, consider how those comments influenced your thoughts. Add that to the right column. A few examples are offered below regarding two responses to someone forming a new boundary.

Person's Name: Their Words	How They Influenced My Thoughts
Addison: "It's not that big of a deal."	I feel minimized. It makes me think my boundaries aren't important to her and that she doesn't care about me.
Bennett: "I'm so happy you shared that with me."	I feel respected. I'm glad I was brave enough to share. We can both benefit from my courage. Setting boundaries can help our relationship.

Person's Name: Their Words	How They Influenced My Thoughts

· · · · · · ·

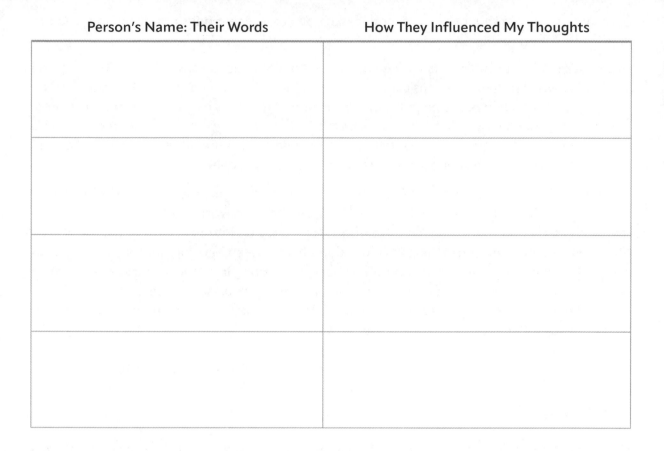 TYPES OF FEEDBACK

The different things that people say to us often fall into similar categories. Here are a few to be aware of.

Supportive: Supportive statements help to motivate you throughout your journey. Encouraging thoughts can help to inspire your self-love, especially in the moments you need it the most. Although these statements can set examples of compassion, they can be difficult to take in if you're not accustomed to hearing them.

Genuine: Genuine statements are shared with honesty and are encapsulated by the best of intentions. Sometimes they're easy to absorb; at other times receiving them can be challenging. This is in part because transparent statements can be hurtful. So if you're in doubt, pause, step back, and revisit the thought in smaller doses. If you determine it does not fit for you, you can always place it aside.

Expectations: Some statements convey the expectation of what you should value. They include suggestions of standards, responsibilities, and obligations. Sometimes they conveniently align with your values and serve as a helpful reminder. In other times they can make you feel pressured. These expectations may help to spark a realization of a previously unacknowledged value and can prompt a recalibration that helps to improve boundaries. On the other hand, others' expectations may conflict with your boundaries, which can drain your energy.

Discriminatory: Prejudiced statements can be draining for your boundaries. These include thoughts that are minimizing and that devalue your intrinsic worth. These incendiary statements can inflict harm on your self-love efforts, can become internalized, and can skew your boundary design. Sometimes these insidious thoughts can seep into your journey without your even realizing it, which can hinder your effectiveness. Investing in self-love and strong personal boundaries can help to buffer some of these remarks. However, biases can be hurtful, regardless of how durable your personal parameters may be. Allow yourself space and grace to process and heal from any inflammatory comments made to you.

. . . .

REFLECTION

Considering how others' thoughts may affect you, where are your opportunities to grow in terms of building boundaries?

_____

_____

_____

_____

HEALING

In our boundary-design journey, some obstacles we encounter may turn into setbacks. During these moments we can become self-critical, judgmental—even mean to ourselves. From a self-loving perspective, setbacks are an inevitable part of the process, and how you respond to those moments often matters more than the fall itself. If we can instead manage to be understanding, compassionate, and kind, we can empower ourselves to propel forward on our path once again. When we encounter a boundary setback, we're likely to reassess the boundary altogether. Even aspects we were confident in come into question. What happened? Is this boundary still important? Is the effort required worthwhile? Sometimes setbacks have a snowball effect. The aftershock of a big setback can bring into question if your boundary is doable or even desirable. The trick is to not let setbacks tempt us to abandon our intention of designing healthy boundaries. Healing is a self-loving choice in which we seek to gather the inertia of a setback and use it to cultivate growth. Healing helps us get up, dust off our hands, and move forward.

REFLECTION

Think about the challenges you've endured in the boundary-design process. In what ways have you been healing? Where do you have opportunities to heal?

CHAPTER 9

BOUNDARY LEVELS

Beyond knowing where your boundaries are needed, it can be helpful to know with whom they apply. Since every situation is different, what you need with one person may look different from what you need with another. Further, in order to establish a strong foundation for successful strategies, you must begin by exploring what boundaries look like with your own self. (See the Boundary Levels worksheet on page 190.) Personal parameters help you infer what interpersonal boundaries need to be formed and how you may benefit from forming them, and your self-respect can model how others can honor your boundaries as well. In this section we'll take a deeper dive into boundary levels and common opportunities for setting boundaries at each juncture.

The framework divides boundaries into three main levels. The first level contains your core boundaries. The next two levels are your interpersonal boundaries. The secondary level contains your closer interpersonal boundaries, such as the relationships you hold with specific people. The tertiary level contains wider social boundaries, the established social systems—with their traditions, rules, cues, and patterns. When people set out to address boundaries, they often focus on the secondary level. But the reality is that your core boundaries are both important and influential—and when core boundaries are overlooked, the boundaries that are created are often poorly designed. As such, let's begin with our core boundaries.

CORE BOUNDARIES

Your core boundaries are your personal parameters—guidelines based on what you need from yourself. From a self-loving perspective, this layer helps you to connect to the deeper meaning of why all the boundaries you need are important.

As the sole creator and recipient of core boundaries, you are privy to all facets of how your boundaries affect you, both when they're maintained and when they're pushed. You've also come to learn the areas that you have thrived in as opposed to the areas that you find challenging. All of these personal lessons help you to improve your boundary knowledge and self-love, which will help you when building subsequent boundaries. Remaining connected to, and intermittently returning and reflecting to this core level, is integral to the healthy boundary-design process. Whereas, neglecting your core could cause cracks in your foundation that will likely affect all your other boundaries. I encourage you to avoid taking your core boundaries for granted. In complex moments (for example, when you are juggling multiple boundary challenges), returning to your core is a self-loving practice that can help you to establish a sense of grounding, a humble acknowledgment of your areas of concern, a recognition of what you can manage, and compassion for yourself and others in the healthy-boundary-design process.

INTERPERSONAL BOUNDARIES

When designing healthy interpersonal boundaries it's important to consider context. To illuminate your present context, take a look at the world around you. What does it look like on a typical day? What spaces do you exist in? Who else shares those spaces? Consider all the relationships you're a part of—and not just with your loved ones. Think about all your interpersonal connections, which of course will vary in proximity, intimacy, and similarity.

Generally speaking, boundaries in peripheral layers are often socially informed. In some ways this is beneficial: rather than needing to negotiate boundaries with every single person in every single context, you can flow with socially accepted stipulations. On the other hand, this can also be tricky. There may be some exceptions in which you yourself or others may not be able to follow along; in addition, not all socially acceptable boundaries are well designed.

For example, when you enter a restaurant and see a line, it's instinctual to get to the back of it to wait your turn. Early years of being taught the function of a waiting line, followed by years of practice and seeing others do the same, sets a wider societal standard. Now, what if the line isn't for ordering food but for the restroom? Let's say you're late for an important meeting, which has been making you nervous for days, and now the butterflies are devolving into an upset stomach. Do you patiently join the end of the line as expected, or do you attempt to succinctly negotiate an exception?

This arbitrary social example may seem simple, but we frequently encounter moments such as these that both affect and are affected by our own boundaries. If you tend to minimize your personal boundaries and you find yourself in line waiting patiently, quietly, and also pressed for time, maybe this would be the last straw for you. But if you're secure in your boundaries with yourself and others, you might be able to offer this person compassion without being threatened.

Though group patterns, practices, and traditions tend to establish stipulations in wider social scenarios, that doesn't mean you can't be an active component in your boundaries at this level. For example, in a family system, there may be a pattern of abuse—and a distinct lack of a boundary—that spans several generations. Since that toxicity likely doesn't align with your values, identity, or wellness, you don't have to be at the mercy of this poorly designed boundary simply because it was maintained by many family members. Nevertheless, choosing to go against the grain can feel like an insurmountable obstacle.

The simplest interpersonal boundary exists between two people. Sometimes just one of the individuals forms the boundary; sometimes both form respective boundaries. But ideally both will collaborate in cocreating the boundary. For example, in planning their wedding, future spouses benefit from considering their mutually respected vows, since these are the tenets their marriage will be based on. Or let's say you're paired with a colleague for a work project. Proactively meeting to assess where you both stand and how you can assist one another in your shared objectives would be a strategic use of your time.

Of course, boundaries can exist between more than two people. While it is possible to form healthy boundaries for multiple people at a time, it can get a bit more complicated given that everyone is unique. Therefore well-designed boundaries for groups should tactfully consider the needs of all while allowing for flexibility and welcoming improvement over time. Generally, school attendance rules require children to be present for each school day. However, exceptions will of course be made for those who are sick or experiencing an emergency.

When appropriate and possible, collaboration should also extend to group boundaries. This often improves representation and widens perspective. Additionally, it may empower individuals to be engaged in the boundary-design process. Those who are connected to the design are likely to be more invested in the overall process. Of course, a drawback of multiple folks collaborating to form a boundary is that it can be challenging to fairly accommodate all needs, preferences, and wishes. But in some cases it's not necessary to expect that one specific boundary will be maintained the same by all involved. From a consistent foundation, boundaries may branch in a group in order to honor individuality.

✏️ FAMILY BOUNDARIES

Recall the case examples you have explored thus far. (See page 57 in chapter 4.) Now, what if I tell you they are all interrelated? Refer to the family diagram to help you answer the questions below.

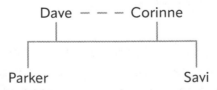

DESIGNING HEALTHY BOUNDARIES

Consider what boundaries may be in place in this family. Keep in mind, boundary breaches are signals of boundaries.

_____

_____

_____

How may some of the family boundaries look different from person to person?

_____

_____

_____

How may these boundaries extend beyond the family? For example, how might Dave have applied these boundaries to Rae? Or how might Corinne have applied them to her friend Maria?

_____

_____

_____

Which boundaries may have been pushed?

_____

_____

_____

Which boundaries can benefit from healing?

_____

_____

_____

There are several iterations to the potential structure, each of which may yield a different under-standing of boundaries. Make your own family rendition using the case examples and create a diagram in the space below. Using that structure, once again explore the questions above. Notice which responses remain consistent and which shift.

_____

_____

_____

_____

_____

_____

. . . .

SOCIAL BOUNDARIES

We typically begin to learn about boundaries as children. We absorb guidelines through explicit guidance as well as from observation. For example, when a parent tells a child to stay away from a hot stove, that explicit guidance is a directly applied boundary. A sibling observing this will likely also adopt that boundary through social learning. Children soak up lessons on what is encouraged and what is discouraged from individuals in all the environments in their life—family, friends, peers, and others in their school and community.

Oftentimes our first boundary lessons focus on what we can or cannot do and why. While these are well-intentioned and often concern safety, to children these parameters often feel more like arbitrary restrictions than helpful guidance. This can set the precedent for children perceiving boundaries as stipulations created by a person in power in order to gain control. Commonly the lesson is conveyed that pushing on a boundary won't just result in the consequences the boundary was intended to prevent—it will bring on punishment as well. In some (unfortunate) cases this punishment comes in the form of shaming or physical abuse. Building on the example above, a caretaker may set the rule to not touch the oven—to protect the child from getting hurt. But let's say the caretaker catches the child reaching for the oven, grabs the child, and then spanks the child; has the boundary been maintained, or breached? Ideally we'll approach boundaries with respect. From a mindset of respect, boundaries balance encouragement and empowerment, prioritize safety and well-being, and are developmentally appropriate. At the onset of life, a child's boundaries are within the care of their guardian(s); as they age, their caretakers scaffold their boundary lessons. By adulthood, they are capable of navigating their boundaries.

When our earliest experience of boundaries are guidelines formed from the basis of respect and love, we're set up to, in turn, create boundaries from the same basis throughout our lifespan. Or, if our earliest experience taught us that boundaries are confusing, conflicting, and intimidating, this assessment can prevail into our adult lives as well. When we're used to boundaries being made *for* us, we can become passive. This passivity can encourage amiability and cooperation— or, if unchecked, it can lead to being taken advantage of. Even when we recognize this fact, it can be a struggle to develop assertiveness if we were not taught how to. In addition, when we're accustomed to boundaries being created solely from outside sources, we can find it difficult to find internal motivation, regulation, connection, and fulfillment.

REFLECTION

What were your first experiences with boundaries? How do those lessons affect you today? What aspects of those initial experiences would you like to maintain? What aspects of those initial experiences would you like to heal from?

While we begin to absorb the world around us in childhood, this continues throughout our lives. Reflecting on these societal insights can help to infer what boundaries already exist around you and where you may need to form additional parameters as well. Zoom out to consider your neighborhood, region, nation, etc. What boundaries already exist in these areas? Where do you see a need for boundaries in these areas?

Consider the social groups you are a part of (family, friends, colleagues, faith, ethnic, etc.). What boundaries already exist in these areas? Where do you see a need for boundaries in these areas?

✏️ EXPLORING SOCIAL BOUNDARIES

Think of three recent news events. Place them in the column on the left. Use the column on the right to reflect on what those events may mean about the boundaries that may or may not exist in society and what boundaries you may wish to form. Two examples are offered below.

Event	Boundary Insights
A snowstorm is expected in a few days.	The city is preparing and I will need to prepare as well. To protect my well-being, I will need to cancel my dinner plans and make time to stock up on supplies. I may need to form temporary work boundaries since it may not be safe for me to leave.

A hate crime was committed against someone who identifies as I do.	The police are looking for the suspects involved. I recognize I have no control over what happens, but I do hope justice is served. I notice that these hate crimes have been increasing and I am scared. I will try to be in the company of others when I am out in public, continue self-defense classes, and advocate for social justice.

✎ MORAL DEVELOPMENT

American psychologist Lawrence Kohlberg theorized that strong morals influence an individual's ability to imbue a sense of ethics and maintain justice. A child in the earliest phase of development is likely to obey authority simply to evade punishment. Obedience is largely based on personal interest—for example, when told to not touch a hot stove. Can you think of another example?

In the second stage of development the older child becomes interested in making choices that can be beneficial to others as well—peers beyond the self. During this stage authority is often still respected, often without question. An example would be a teammate showing up to practice on time out of respect to their teammates. Can you think of another example?

In the final stage, individuals are capable of seeing not only the perspective of those they care about but also that of others in general. In this phase, universal ethics steer moral principles. From this conceptualization, the individual is likely to view healthy boundaries as highly valuable—not just as protections specific to one person or another. For example, let's say someone finds a wallet in a hotel lobby and takes it to the reception desk. They might do so not just because they don't want to be accused of theft or because they expect a reward in return, but because they feel morally obligated to do so. Can you think of another example?

· · · · · · ·

COMMON BOUNDARY LEVELS

Boundary levels concern the intersection of people and places. Exploring where your boundary levels exist calls for considering all of the people and places you encounter in your life. Before you complete the following activity, it might be helpful to revisit Identity Roles on page 69.

✏️ COMMON BOUNDARY LEVELS: PEOPLE

The chart below lists people you may wish to form boundaries with. If a suggestion applies to you, check the box on the left, then add those people's names to the column on the right. Feel free to add additional relationships in the blank lines.

Partners	
Parents, stepparents, and guardians	
Children, nieces, and nephews	
Siblings	
Grandparents	
Grandchildren	
In-laws	

Aunts and uncles	
Cousins	
Other family members	
Friends	
Acquaintances	
Classmates	
Coworkers	
Teammates	
Neighbors	
Teachers	
Coaches	
Managers	
Supervisors	
Supervisees	
Employers	

Employees		
Physicians		
Attorneys		
Clients		
Patients		
Customers		

Some of the people you've identified may warrant explicitly defined boundaries (such as business partners), whereas others may largely rely on wider societal parameters unless otherwise needed. As you begin designing boundaries, it can be helpful to prioritize personal parameters before subsequently delving into the interpersonal boundaries that carry more weight in your life. You may find that the parameters you initially address can help to set the precedent for the peripheral boundaries. Say, for example, you reflect on your financial wellness and decide to set parameters to pay off your debt. Establishing grounding parameters can help you to be more mindful about the choices you make in a variety of contexts. Your personal boundaries will likely support particular spending and saving habits that can affect the decisions you make in other levels. It may influence how you choose to eat from day to day, the gifts you give, and whom you spend your time with.

· · · · · · ·

Next we'll want to consider boundaries of place, since part of designing healthy boundaries concerns where you may need them. For example, being exposed to diverse environments can help us to learn about others' boundaries—as well as give us perspective about the boundaries of our own cultures. Our foundational boundaries tend to expand to our social sphere, from the teacher who helps us learn to the schoolmate who sits with us on the bus. Over time you pick up cues and adapt accordingly, sometimes without conscious thought. For example, you'd have completely different clothing, behavior, and demeanor at a funeral than you would at a wedding.

Generally speaking, the boundaries you maintain with a particular person vary from situation to situation. For example, though intimate partners would likely exhibit different physical boundaries in their own home than they would in public, the basis of those boundaries would nevertheless be relatively consistent.

When incorporating wider societal parameters such as social expectations, common practices, cultural traditions, policies, guidelines, and laws, it can be helpful to consider different environments. For example, when you enter a train station, you don't need to set boundaries with each person you encounter, since the general boundaries we have with strangers are already in place. Boundaries in social situations tend to include what is traditional, common, and culturally accepted in that environment. Oftentimes these parameters have been in place well beyond your years and have been communally upheld beyond your own self. Considering the power that upholds these tenets, you have the privilege of safety when they align with your personal parameters—or you may risk friction, conflict, and even danger if they do not. For example, different regions have laws in place regarding what behavior is acceptable (a right to be upheld) and what is banned. If your personal parameters don't align with communal ones, strengthening your personal boundaries may be warranted.

✎ COMMON BOUNDARY LEVELS: PLACES

While considering boundaries for every environment you step into might feel overwhelming, the reality is that you need boundaries in all situations. Scenarios in any space can be better balanced with boundary awareness. In the box below you'll find some sample spaces that you may benefit from exploring boundaries in. Circle all the ones that apply to you. Add an asterisk next to those that are a part of your daily life. Flag in particular (perhaps with an arrow) any unique spaces that warrant boundary investment due to their special circumstances. Feel free to add your own as well.

Bathroom	Living Room	Wedding
Bedroom	Park	Work
Bus	Place of worship	_____
Car	Plane	_____
Class	Post Office	_____
Community center	Restaurant	_____
Dinner party	School	_____
Doctor's office	Stadium	_____
Graduation ceremony	Store	_____
Gym	Theater	_____
Home	Train	_____
Kitchen	University	_____

• • • • • • •

COLLABORATIVE BOUNDARIES

As noted previously, one of the common pitfalls of the boundary process is that we view boundaries as a system of defense. This stems from the perception of boundaries as being one-directional. While this may be the case in some instances, it's helpful to note that some of the best boundaries are cocreated. Considering the person(s) to whom the boundary applies can help to form a more purposeful parameter. Within healthy connections, this can actually add an ease to the boundary-design journey, since you can benefit from support and experience camaraderie in the process. Collaborative boundary formation can also assist in shedding light on individualistic blind spots, expanding perspectives, and healing through boundary challenges.

Admittedly, it can seem daunting to consider others' priorities in addition to your own. Also, it's not always an easy process to codesign boundaries, especially in scenarios in which there is past strife, contrasting priorities, and stark differences of opinion. For example, establishing new boundaries with one's fiancé is very different from redefining boundaries after getting a divorce. That being said, reflecting on these types of boundaries can make for more realistic, just boundaries in the long run.

Collaborative boundaries are especially important when there are dual relationships. This is when each person holds more than one role. Examples include a best friend who is also your coworker, a cousin who is also your coach, and a business partner who is also your sibling. When two people bring their own past, present, and future to the table in boundary creation it can be complicated, so you can imagine that in dual relationships there is an added layer of complexity. Boundaries from the original relationship may or may not easily carry over to the next; also, boundaries that are not essential in the former may be important in the latter. Another time that collaborative boundaries are a priority is when a relationship progresses and a new condition, phase, or experience may warrant boundary reconsideration, such as moving in together, traveling, or going into business together.

While we tend to overlook the need for collaborative boundaries in general, we do so especially in dual relationships, since we can fail to see the wider realm of the roles we hold with others and that they hold with us in turn. We may also presume that the mere existence of established boundaries should withstand the evolution of the relationship. While core boundaries may last throughout a bond, they can always benefit from being revisited and attuned.

REFLECTION

Revisit the previous two activities regarding people and places. Can you identify any collaborative boundaries that are already in place? Do you see opportunities for creating new collaborative boundaries?

CHAPTER 10

CREATING HEALTHY BOUNDARIES

Before we head into the process of boundary creation, let's take a moment to reflect.

REFLECTION

At this point in your boundary journey, you've explored a variety of aspects of the process, including key components, likely obstacles, and where and with whom boundaries may be needed. Throughout this book, you have likely noticed what you may need for the path ahead. Use the space below to reflect on how you may want to prepare for the journey ahead. You may find it helpful to glance back at previous chapters to refresh your memory. For example:

- I would like to practice more self-kindness.
- I hope to expand my support system.
- I plan to reflect on my core values.

THE DESIGN PROCESS

Again, the boundary-design process encompasses creation, assertion, and healing. As you already know, the process calls for a great deal of reflection, which occurs throughout the journey. A thoughtful approach to core boundaries helps to maximize on healthy boundary design. In turn, this method enhances your ability to better withstand what will come your way in the future. Attuned awareness at every phase will help you to assess your equilibrium.

In this chapter, we'll address creating the boundaries you've been preparing for. Thanks to your work exploring boundary domains and levels, we'll have a clear sense of what you wish to cultivate and protect—as well as what you wish to release and repel. Based on the depth of work you've done so far, the necessary boundaries and respective potential effects begin to surface.

In chapter 11, the setting phase, we incorporate methods of communicating boundaries and bring them to fruition—thereby putting our boundaries into action.

Ideally, well-designed boundaries are received with ease and can be sustained for a length of time. But know that it is more common for boundaries to require multiple attempts of being communicated and emphasized, and so, in the final phase, it is paramount that support be maintained until each boundary is fully accepted. However, even the best of boundary designs can warrant healing at some point—sooner or later. For example, you may have honed solid wellness routines but a pandemic shakes your stable system. Additionally, this phase may encompass your own reception of others' boundaries, as well as your strategies to respect boundaries in tandem. Ultimately, this "healing" phase isn't just about restoring and strengthening the boundaries you've set so that you can protect what matters most to you; it's also about helping you to incorporate forgiveness in times of difficulty and to practice self-love as you persevere in your journey.

CREATING BOUNDARIES

All the boundaries you will form are established on a basis of your beliefs about boundaries. Before considering the core and peripheral parameters you have in your life, you need to revisit and connect to a general understanding of what boundaries are, what they mean to you, and why they are important. As you tailor boundaries throughout your life, you'll return to this space to ground yourself before taking an additional step on your path.

REFLECTION

What do boundaries mean to you at this juncture? (Feel free to flip back to earlier chapters and revisit your definitions from previous reflections, including in particular the one on page 13.)

_____

_____

_____

_____

✎ RETURNING TO YOUR BASE

Returning to the reflection above can form a base for you to recalibrate throughout the boundary-design process. Additionally, you can expand your base by creating a safe zone for you to return to when challenged throughout the journey. For some, this may be a physical location with tangible items, such as a comfortable corner of a bedroom with a drawer filled with self-care items like a journal, essential oils, and treasured pictures. For others, it may be a place within you that you can reach by methods such as deep breathing, contemplation, meditation, or prayer.

What would you like to incorporate in your base?

_____

_____

_____

How will you know when you need to return to your base?

_____

_____

_____

_____

ASSESSING BOUNDARIES

After connecting to the purpose that motivates your boundary-design journey, you can revisit the work you've done assessing where boundaries are warranted and with whom they are needed. Revisit chapters 5 to 9 on boundary domains and levels to assist you in proceeding.

HIGHLIGHTING CORE BOUNDARIES

While boundary domains and levels may vary from person to person, the first boundary level is relatively constant for us all. This is your core boundary level. It encompasses the boundaries you have with yourself based on your boundary domains. When you revisit the four core questions in chapters 5 through 8, what you want your boundaries to cultivate and protect, as well as what you hope to release and repel, will begin to surface. These become the foundation of your personal and interpersonal boundaries. What you establish at this layer will inform the parameters you set with others. For example, over time, you may receive consistent messaging from loved ones that sheds light on a blind spot of yours. When you recognize that this information forms a pattern, you may wish to integrate that feedback to further bolster your core boundaries.

✎ CONNECTING TO YOUR CORE

Revisit the reflections and activities in the boundary domain chapters (chapters 5 through 8), especially the My Core Values chart on page 79. Now we're going to expand your assessment. In the blank chart on pages 142 and 143 for each boundary domain, consider what you wish to cultivate and protect. Next, explore what you hope to let go of, as well as what you want to shield yourself from. To offer some examples, a sample chart precedes your blank chart. (Note that we cover similar terrain with the Your Boundary Code worksheet in the appendix on page 191.)

	Cultivate and Protect	Release and Repel
Who are you	• Cultural traditions • Quality family time • Career growth	• Prejudice and discrimination • Negative self-talk • Toxic influences

	Cultivate and Protect	Release and Repel
What do you believe?	• Authenticity, kindness, and love are integral • People have the power to learn and grow	• People-pleasing • Judgmental opinions
How do you find balance?	• Mental health is a priority • Me time • Reading	• Imbalanced relationships • Eating habits that are unkind to my body
Where do you have the opportunity to grow?	• Patience • Healthy relationships	• Impulsivity • Rushing • Prioritizing others' schedules over my own

CONNECTING TO YOUR CORE CHART

	Cultivate and Protect	Release and Repel
Who are you?		
What do you believe?		

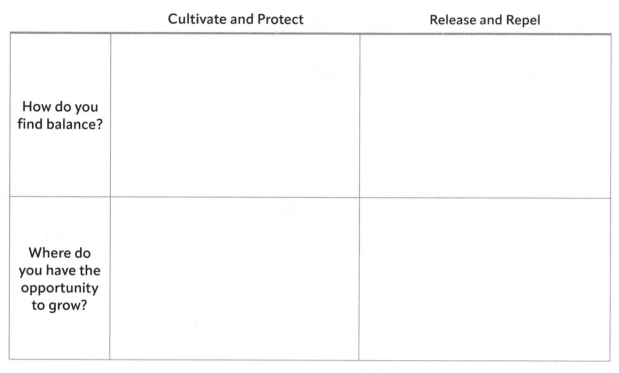

	Cultivate and Protect	Release and Repel
How do you find balance?		
Where do you have the opportunity to grow?		

. . . .

EXPLORING CORE BOUNDARIES

Your core boundaries are the guidelines that help you to turn the details on your chart into a reality. Within each box in the table you just filled you can find spools of thread that can be sewn into strong boundaries. When you step back and take in what you want to foster and what you wish to protect yourself from, the pattern of what you wish to weave will surface.

To follow are some personal boundaries that could arise from the sample chart:

- I will not condone negative statements.
- I will not tolerate prejudice or discrimination.
- I will respect my time.
- I plan to fuel my body with sufficient nutrition and hydration.
- I will allow myself to pause.
- I will give myself permission to take breaks.
- I will honor my energy levels.

- I will allow myself to slow down.
- I will embrace learning.
- I will caution investing energy in one-sided connections.
- I hope to learn from my mistakes.
- I want to be gentle with myself during challenging times.
- I will make time for my loved ones.
- I will practice traditions that connect me to my culture.
- I will value my mental health.
- I will be honest with myself.
- I welcome kind honesty from others.
- I will practice kindness.
- I will invest in purposeful relationships.
- I hope to respect my time and others'.

✎ EXPLORING YOUR CORE BOUNDARIES

Using the Connecting to Your Core chart (pages 142 to 143), explore your personal boundaries in the space below.

_____

_____

_____

_____

_____

_____

_____

_____

_____

_____

· · · · · · ·

In chapter 6 you refined your core values by Exploring Your Value Code (page 74), Refining Your Ranking (page 76), and Decoding Your Values (page 77). Similarly, your core boundaries can be refined by coalescing like elements. Review the personal boundaries you just explored and make a note of the themes you find there. To better elucidate your core boundaries you can combine the like items in your personal boundaries, clarify their connection to each other, and solidify your intentions in a core boundary statement.

One of the themes that can be seen in the bullet list of sample boundaries (see page 143) is time. That theme could be exemplified in the following sample core boundaries:

I intend to respect my time. I will check in with my energy levels, and when needed, I will allow myself to slow down, pause, and take breaks. I will invest time to fuel my body, mental health, and relationships. I will give myself time to pace myself and grow as I learn to respect my time and others'.

✎ CORE BOUNDARY STATEMENTS

Use the space below to explore your core boundary statements.

_____

_____

_____

_____

_____

_____

_____

_____

· · · · · · ·

STRENGTHENING YOUR CORE

For each core boundary statement that you've made, consider specific details that would help you to honor your personal boundaries. You may find it helpful to utilize visualization (see the Visualization: Intentions activity on page 103) to help you imagine what it could look like when you're connected to your core.

Building on the time boundary explored in the example above, sample details could include:

- I hope to check in with my energy levels 2x per day.
- When I notice a strong emotion (e.g., anger), I will allow myself a moment to check in with myself.
- I will reflect on what it looks like when I need to slow down, pause, and take a break.
- I will be mindful of obstacles (e.g., people-pleasing) that keep me from respecting my time.
- I will connect with others who value my time.
- I will make plans with people who want to _____.
- I hope to visit the market just once a week.
- I will attend weekly therapist appointments.
- I hope to be active at least 3 days a week.
- I will host a cultural celebration this year.
- I would like to organize a monthly family get-together.
- I will learn how my loved ones want to spend our time together.

✎ STRENGTHENING YOUR CORE

Use the space below to explore strategies to implement in your life so as to strengthen your core.

_____

_____

_____

_____

_____

· · · · · · ·

PERIPHERAL BOUNDARIES

As explored in chapter 9, boundaries occur on multiple levels, beginning with your core boundaries at the foundational level. Your core boundaries may be used as a guideline to establish subsequent boundaries, giving you a grounding point to inform your collaboration, respect, and protection with others. Now, when you take into consideration all of the people and places boundaries are warranted, it's easy to feel overwhelmed. However, considering that the absence of a boundary is still a pathway, the reality is that there *are* boundaries at each of these intersections. These are peripheral boundaries. Just take one level at a time.

You may find it resourceful to begin will common contexts, the spaces you find yourself in and whom you may encounter in those areas. Another method is to prioritize the levels that are most meaningful to you. Neither strategy suggest that one level is more important the other; they are merely method to help you progress in forming peripheral parameters of protection.

Over time, as you establish and practice peripheral boundaries, the process will feel easier to you. And with each boundary level you address, your experience will help to build your confidence, awareness, and knowledge. With this engaged process, even if an unexpected boundary level pops up from your blind spot, your commitment to the process will help you to quickly address it.

✎ MAPPING PERIPHERAL BOUNDARIES

Use the figures of concentric circles below to map your boundary levels. Two sets are provided in the appendix on page 193 to offer you the chance to try the two strategies delineated above. You may find it helpful to reference the boundary levels you explored in chapter 9.

Example:

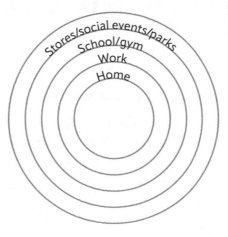

Stores/social events/parks
School/gym
Work
Home

· · · · · · ·

✎ EXPLORING YOUR PERIPHERAL BOUNDARIES

This exercise will build on the foundation of your core boundaries to explore your peripheral boundaries below. For each theme, you will provide a core statement then in chart form provide at least one example from your common boundary domains. Here is a sample exploration:

Core boundary statement regarding the theme of: time

I intend to respect my time. I will check in with my energy levels, and when needed, I will allow myself to slow down, pause, and take breaks. I will invest time to fuel my body, mental health, and relationships. I will give myself time to pace myself and grow as I learn to respect my time and others'.

Level	Boundary
Home	I will invest time in creating and maintaining a clean and comfortable environment.
School	I will work slowly on assignments to avoid feeling overwhelmed at the end.
Work	I will check in with my energy levels during my shift and take breaks.
Gym	I will try to make time to work out one to three times per week.
Stores	I will make a list of the items I need so I can make my shopping trips more efficient.
Social	I will check in with my energy before attending a social event.
Parks	When I am feeling overwhelmed I will make time to visit the park.
Partner	I will prioritize time with my partner.
Family	I hope to plan a family gathering once a month.
Friends	I will offer time to the friends who value my energy.
Colleagues	I will pay attention to the signs that I need to take a break from work.
Acquaintances	I will not force myself to attend events if I do not have the time or energy.
Neighbors	I aim to allow myself time to get to know my neighbors.
Strangers	I want to practice patience with everyone I come across.

· · · · · · ·

CHAPTER 11

SETTING HEALTHY BOUNDARIES

When you enact a personal boundary for yourself or when you communicate an interpersonal boundary to others, this gives momentum to the goals you have set for yourself. But before you do that, it can be helpful to thoroughly consider what you want to convey and to take steps to ensure you feel safe in doing so.

CONSIDERATIONS TO MAKE BEFORE SETTING BOUNDARIES

Before you transition boundaries from concept to practice, you'll want to consider a few essential details, including what you want to share, whom you want to share with, how you want to share, and the consequences of sharing. Complete the worksheet Setting Boundaries on page 196 of the appendix.

CONSIDER YOUR CORE

Since a healthy-design process is infused with self-love, a key way to honor yourself as you set a parameter is by prioritizing your core. Revisiting your core boundaries can help to remind you of who you are, what matters most to you, and why. This reminder serves as a compass to guide you as you put your boundary in place.

Before contemplating how you will communicate a boundary to another person, remember that how you establish and maintain your personal boundaries provides a sturdy foundation for how you establish and maintain peripheral boundaries.

Prior to putting your boundaries in place, be sure to walk the walk. Vow to honor and respect your boundaries the same way you wish others will honor and respect yours. Committing to this intention thus offers a foundation from which to communicate your boundaries. To follow are some questions to help you convey your boundaries.

What type of firmness do you tend to gravitate to for boundaries? Why do you believe you are drawn to this approach? What boundaries would you like to be more firm with? What would be needed to make that change? What boundaries would you like to be more flexible with? What would be needed to make that change?

_____

_____

_____

_____

_____

CONSIDER WHAT YOU WANT TO SHARE

In some instances, the best way to fortify a boundary is by providing clear details about it, such as the experiences that led you to forming it, its purpose, examples of what it would look like, and the conditions of honoring it. Additional details may be useful if the boundary is particularly detailed or complicated—say, there's a sharp contrast between what life looks like with and without it—or, better yet, if the recipient is willing to collaborate in the process. Emotions are influential in memory formation and learning. If you're willing to touch on the emotional reasons you want to set a boundary, caring recipients will better understand its importance and will want to learn how you'd like it to be respected.

I want to clarify the fact that, just because you've gathered a wealth of information about what boundaries you want to create and why, that doesn't mean you're required to disclose all this information. There may be instances when no words will suffice, in which case you might simply remove yourself from the situation without saying anything. If doing this would be unusual for you, this unexpected change in behavior may convey your message without words. This could be preferable when you don't want to share your underlying purpose, when your boundary has been overstepped previously (especially with that particular person), or when the recipient is unable to tolerate and/or comprehend the depth of your boundary.

Note that on occasion you might alter your initial approach. Let's say you initially feel vulnerable disclosing details about your boundary, and so you opt for communicating it concisely. However, if over time you notice that the boundary is consistently overstepped, you may reevaluate how best to relay to the recipient why this boundary is important to you. We'll cover this in the following chapter. Or, sometimes you may begin with a concise request in an emergency and then elaborate on it at a later time. For example, when I was in the middle of writing this book, my son was rushed to the hospital overnight. Though I needed to inform my colleagues and clients of my absence, it was unnecessary for me to provide details on why—and I didn't yet know for how long. So I sent a quick, succinct email telling them I would be unavailable for the time being and would be in touch again when I could.

Here's an example of another reason to limit the information you share.

🗀 GERARD

Gerard narrowly avoided a fatal accident while driving under the influence. In the days following, he did some soul-searching about the severity of his alcoholism and his chances of getting, and staying, sober. This formidable goal was further challenged by the fact that most of the people in his social support system drink alcohol, and most of the time they spend together involves drinking. If Gerard were to get sober, he'd have to set up a boundary between himself and alcohol—which also calls for a boundary between himself and his circle. Gerard would prefer to keep his quandary to himself until he makes a decision. But if he doesn't share it, he may find himself in situations where he's tempted or even pressured to drink with his friends. So Gerard considers sharing that he's *thinking* about sobriety. If that goes well, he'd likely get less pressure from his circle—and maybe even gain some support.

How does this example apply to you? In an analogous situation of your own, you may opt to keep your quandary to yourself until you're clear on what you need—or, you may choose to convey the evolving nature of the boundary. This consideration is particularly helpful when you're new to the boundary-design process, when the specific boundary is new, and/or if the topic area is challenging for you.

CONSIDER WHOM YOU WANT TO SHARE WITH

The previous anecdote regarding Gerard exemplifies why you don't need to communicate every boundary you make with every human you encounter. For each boundary, consider who needs to hear it, and why.

Start by considering who should be offered the most information. Examples include people you are close to, people who can collaborate with you and support you, and people whom the boundary most impacts—those who will have a direct shift in their perceptions, behavior, and dynamics as a result. In Gerard's case, this would include anyone who might expect to share a drink with him. Next, consider common societal boundaries, which are informed by laws, ethics, and communal practices. In some cases disclosure would be less warranted—or perhaps redundant or even inappropriate.

🗀 RAE

Having an affinity for animals and a passion for conservation, Rae has wanted to become a marine biologist since childhood. But an early diagnosis of dyslexia meant that interests in learning were often overshadowed by its challenges. Rae succeeded in getting accepted into grad school, but found the rigorous reading and writing required for the dissertation particularly daunting. Dr. Clifton, Rae's mentor, has observed a decrease in both the quality and quantity of Rae's writing, and scheduled a meeting to discuss her concerns.

Rae knows that support could be extremely helpful but has always kept the diagnosis private out of fear of being treated differently—or, worse, being penalized somehow, or rejected altogether.

If you were in Rae shoes, what would you do? Would you want to tell someone? If so, whom?

_____

_____

_____

_____

_____

· · · · · · ·

CONSIDER HOW YOU WANT TO SHARE

After thinking about what you want to communicate about your boundary and with whom, next consider how you wish to share. This decision can be informed by what parts of the boundary you wish to share, your history with boundaries, and your experiences with the recipient.

Your first option is to not share at all. Perhaps your information is personal, private, sensitive, or complex. Or maybe timing is an issue; you may choose to wait until your disclosure would be warranted. It's certainly true that untimely conveyance, such as when telling someone when they're under duress, can impede communication and ultimately hinder the boundary. You may

DESIGNING HEALTHY BOUNDARIES

opt to communicate your boundary by simply putting it into action yourself; without words, the boundary can be received through the ripple effects of your modeling.

On the other side of the spectrum, you may opt for direct communication. The best medium to choose—whether digital or actual, textual or visual or in person—will vary based on the context. When communicating simple boundaries such as preferring to reserve Friday evenings for time to yourself, an impersonal method such as a text may suffice. For times when documentation would be beneficial, an email or letter might be called for. A letter is ideal when you're requesting a firm, formal boundary with someone. For any more personal situations with people you care about, especially scenarios involving emotions, I encourage you to communicate in person if at all possible, or via video call at minimum. It's so easy for people to misinterpret another's intention, tone, or message, and your body language and energy can help to convey your sincerity and good intentions if the recipient doesn't respond well.

Of course, since boundaries can be needed in difficult situations, feelings such as frustration, confusion, and anger can seep into your communication. Again, scenarios like this can often best be handled face to face, since in-person communication conveys your commitment to the relationship regardless of the negative emotions in the mix. I do caution that you do your best to regulate your emotions before proceeding—and I definitely don't recommend passive-aggressive methods such as posting on social media, gossiping, or ghosting.

Boundaries can be a challenging investment. Considering the context of the boundary in question can help you determine the method of sharing that will work best for you. When at all possible, seek an environment that makes you feel calm, clear, and balanced.

🗀 SAVI

You may recall (from page 36) that Savi experienced trauma in her senior year of high school. In the years since, she never told anyone about it. Ten years on, Savi has committed to her healing journey in a variety of ways, including yoga, therapy, and support groups. Within the last year, Savi has been working on designing healthier boundaries.

The highlight of Savi's Tuesday is her yoga class, to which she always arrives early. While unrolling her mat she notices a new instructor, who flashes a kind smile. Shortly after, the instructor announces, "I'll be offering hands-on adjustments for your practice today. If that's not your thing, just gimme a shout." A few classmates chuckle and one exclaims, "Who wouldn't want that?!" Well, Savi doesn't want hands-on anything. Yoga is Savi's safe place. It's where she has made the most progress in healing, including through her history of body dysmorphia and social anxiety. She is instantly triggered and overwhelmed. Which is worse: letting a stranger adjust her poses, or shouting to the class that that's not "her thing"? Both the announcement and the banter in the room spark a spiral of shame in her.

Let's apply what you've learned to the above scenario. Savi's first job is to decide whether she wants to share at all. Despite her distress, a decade of investing in her healing has motivated her to speak up for herself when needed, so she decides to bite the bullet and honor her commitment to herself. Next, she has to consider *how* she wishes to share.

In the chart Communicating Your Boundary on page 198, Savi might choose speaking out publicly in class, telling the instructor before class starts, and calling the studio after class as potential options to address her boundary concern.

If you were in Savi's shoes, how would you address this boundary? Share the rationale behind your selection(s). We'll return to this scenario on page 155.

_____

_____

_____

_____

_____

· · · · · · ·

CONSIDER THE CONSEQUENCES

Lastly, before putting a boundary in place it can be helpful to consider the reverberations that may ripple from it. Some may surface as gentle, welcoming vibrations—while others might be more tectonic. Weighing the potential risks can help you to recognize the value of the boundary and your dedication to the process. It can also inform the strategies you might use to ease the process. Examples of negative effects include prompting a challenge, eliciting an argument, feeling disrespected, or losing a connection. While one might want to avoid risking any of the above, at the same time there are potential benefits as well, including prompting growth for yourself/others, deepening a bond, and feeling proud and grateful. Ultimately, this reflection helps you to prepare—and potentially gather additional resources to bolster your continued process.

While the breadth in this assessment can seem daunting, keep in mind that the purpose of proactive contemplation is to enhance your empowerment. The intention is not to control the path—but to better travail it. When you find yourself at a fork in the road, knowing how to consider your options before proceeding can help you make an informed decision equipped with the resources needed for the journey ahead.

DESIGNING HEALTHY BOUNDARIES

When addressing details such as what, who, how, why, and when, deeply consider the pros and cons of each available option. As you move through the process and narrow down your choices, it may aid your decision to do what's called a SWOT (Strengths, Weaknesses, Opportunities, and Threats) analysis. For more, see the Take a SWOT activity to follow.

📁 SAVI—To recollect what we know about Savi, see pages 36 and 153.

Savi has been using the healthy-design process in her healing journey for a few years. So, even though she's triggered by the incident at the yoga class, she's still able to recover quickly enough to consider her options. Given that she's been working on building her self-esteem, she knows that advocating for herself is a great way to cultivate confidence. She's also been looking to challenge her growth with real-life opportunities as they arise, and here's her chance to practice effective communication, assertiveness, and emotional regulation. She recognizes the strength of speaking her piece and is leaning toward approaching the instructor before class starts. On the other hand, she still feels ashamed. What if her going up to talk to the instructor gets noticed by others? Their quick, boisterous banter makes her worried they might mock her, and she'll feel dismissed, jeered—even humiliated. That would ruin the class for her. She might not even feel comfortable at that studio anymore—which would be a huge setback. Losing her primary form of self-care, even temporarily, till she found another studio she likes, would take a toll on her well-being.

How does Savi's assessment compare with yours? You may have considered more details, especially since you have the luxury of time—as well as distance from Savi's emotional history. Savi's assessment could certainly be more in depth. But remember that she had to swiftly implementing a SWOT analysis on the fly. If she'd had more time, she could have considered additional details for each domain, elicited feedback, and sought support. In any case, she can revisit and refine her assessment when she enters the healing phase of boundary design.

✏️ TAKE A SWOT

Think of a boundary you're in the process of forming. Use the SWOT chart to further explore it in relation to your strengths, weaknesses, opportunities, and threats. You'll also find a SWOT chart in the appendix on page 197.

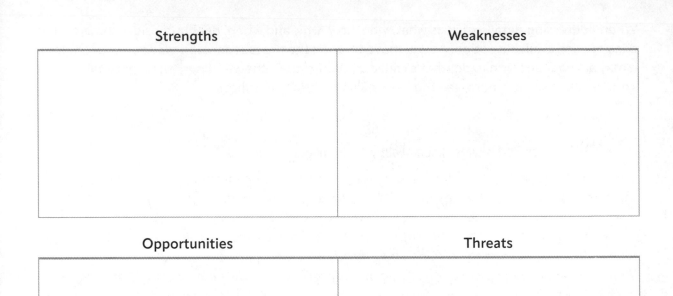

Strengths	Weaknesses

Opportunities	Threats

INFUSING SELF-LOVE INTO THE BOUNDARY-SETTING PROCESS

As it happens, you do have the luxury of time and distance (from Savi's decision, at least). As you progress in your boundary-setting process, there are a number of ways you can infuse self-love throughout—namely: know your truth, reverse roles, strive for balance, apply pace and patience, practice, walk the walk, and seek support.

KNOW YOUR TRUTH

Self-love helps you to connect to your truth, which can serve as a compass throughout your boundary-design journey. Before being able to set clear, healthy boundaries, you have to believe in your ability to do so in order to invest the energy to do so. Self-awareness is paramount as you consider how to incorporate your strengths, where you can continue to grow, and what you may need to support you in the process. Self-exploration assists you in reflecting on your prior experiences to inform your founding of a new boundary. You're thus able to recognize, and subsequently build upon, your past encounters. Self-love also reminds you that things, people, and contexts can change over time—and so each unique instance can merit a fresh assessment.

REFLECTION

What have your experiences been like setting boundaries?

_____

_____

What have you found challenging about setting boundaries?

_____

_____

What aspects of setting boundaries come easily for you?

_____

_____

What has helped you to set boundaries?

_____

_____

What would you like to improve to help you set healthy boundaries?

_____

_____

REVERSE ROLES

Self-love isn't selfish. Loving yourself helps you to better see, respect, and care for others. When you are setting boundaries, this thoughtfulness can ultimately benefit your boundary design. Rather than solely considering your needs, motivations, and intentions, you're able to make space for others' as well. One way to practice this boundary-informed empathy is to switch your perspective. Put yourself in the recipient's position; from that vista, you can contemplate what may help to establish the boundary.

To expand on the recipient's point of view, recall times when you were the recipient of someone else's boundary. What assisted you in receiving it? Perhaps it was the setting in which they shared it, or the wording they chose. Maybe it was the tone they conveyed, or the conversational approach they used. Everyone is different, and contexts and boundaries vary, but exploring what helped you receive a boundary can help to inform your setting strategies.

Taking someone else's perspective into consideration can also help to combat the standard defensiveness that, when unwarranted, tends to hinder boundaries. The establisher's position can become an impassioned, strong one. While of course everyone has a right to advocate for their boundaries, if that energy isn't properly harnessed it can become unnecessarily aggressive, and may backfire. Using forceful language is not a productive default response. Fortunately, boundaries *can* be formed with politeness, kindness, and care. If it feels right for you, "please" and "thank you" can go a long way. Reversing roles in the boundary-setting phase can assist in forming collaborative, respectful boundaries.

REFLECTION

Reflect on times when boundaries were set with you. Explore what may have helped and/or hindered your ability to receive the boundary, and how that experience may inform your general boundary-setting preferences.

STRIVE FOR BALANCE

Self-care is essential throughout the boundary-design process. Taking care of yourself helps you to gain your footing as you put your boundaries into place. Committing to self-care helps you to clarify your present needs and, thus, what boundaries you may benefit from creating. Being grounded helps you to maintain a connection to your core, improve your mental clarity, and calmly convey your boundaries. As you convey your points, it's important to be kind, calm, attentive, and open in the process. If you do not embody these traits, it's likely that the assertiveness you wish to convey could instead be perceived more as passiveness or aggressiveness.

Although you previously prepared by reflecting on the other person's possible perspectives, in order to maintain balance you must allow the other person the space to share their views as well. Try your best to maintain eye contact and convey your sincerity with a collected tone. While they're speaking, don't use the time to selfishly plan your debate. Instead, actively listen to what they share. Keep in mind that discussing a boundary is not about right or wrong. It's a self-loving process in which you advocate for both your growth and the growth of those around you.

APPLY PACE AND PATIENCE

In the setting phase, pacing and patience are essential forms of self-care. While there is no perfect timing in boundary setting, the right time is informed by your readiness. When you attune to your rhythm, you can utilize this data to inform healthy boundary design. Do you feel prepared to establish your boundary? The formula for your pace may incorporate multiple elements, such as your past experiences with boundary design, the importance of the given boundary, and who is affected by it. Pacing helps you to discern if you need to pause your momentum in order to reflect and seek firmer ground. It also helps you to recognize when you're equipped to press on again. Additionally, if you become flustered when moving to action, pacing can help you to step back and regroup.

In some instances, such as emergency boundaries, you may feel the need to apply rash boundaries and understandably deprioritize pace. However, parameters set in fight-or-flight mode may not be ideal in the long term. Fortunately, post-setting reflection can help you to assess your needs, the context, and the boundary, and a return to pacing can help you to recover.

Paying attention to pacing helps you to foster patience. Giving yourself the space to slow down can help you to improve your tact in the process. It can allow you the time to ground and tap into self-love. Being mindful of your combined readiness and timing also helps you to extend this grace to others—which ultimately enhances your boundary design. While there may be times when someone barges past your boundary with malicious intent, there are plenty of reasons why someone might give your parameter an innocent push. Perhaps the person wants to respect the boundary but misinterpreted it, or perhaps the person lacks bandwidth and is overwhelmed, distracted by a priority of their own. Of course, others' emotional regulation is not your responsibility; the only person you can manage is yourself. However, consideration in the boundary-setting phase can help to improve boundary acknowledgment. Moreover, this understanding has the potential to both assist future boundary setting and enhance the overall relationship dynamic. Examples of patience in the setting phase include allowing space for questions and giving the other person time to process and absorb the depth of your message. This patience reduces the risk of miscommunication, which can often occur if the process is rushed. Offering patience eases pressure, reduces defensiveness, and serves as a catalyst for receptivity. As you can imagine, patience is especially helpful in collaborative boundaries.

It's also true that pacing and patience may not come easily to you. Your eagerness and motivation to design healthy boundaries may push you forward faster than is ideal. If this sounds like you, cultivating these essential self-care skills can benefit your boundary design—as well as your overall well-being.

✎ PACING AND PATIENCE

Take a moment to cultivate pacing and patience by filling in the chart below.

	What are some signs that you may need to:	How can you practice patience during this time?
Keep going		
Pick up speed		
Slow down		
Pause		

PRACTICE

As with the entire boundary-design process, perfection is not our goal. Even with thorough exploration, hard work, and the best of intentions, flubs are part of the journey. If this seems disheartening, consider shifting your mindset. The healthiest of boundaries are not those that are set perfectly; they are the ones set through genuine, aligned action in which there was space for learning, growth, and resilience. Taking on the humble perspective of a lifetime learner permits you to offer your best effort in setting boundaries and to utilize opportunities for growth as challenging yet ultimately fulfilling experiences.

One way to adapt to this frame of mind is to be open to practice. When setting a boundary, give yourself permission to prepare. Write out what you wish to say, practice speaking aloud what you hope to convey, solicit feedback from trusted people in your support system, and seek additional resources when needed. Allow yourself the time and space to practice before setting the initial boundary as well as each time you revisit it.

WALK THE WALK

Practice in the boundary-setting phase can also take the form of consistency. Doing so offers the ability to demonstrate what the boundary looks like and, more specifically, what it looks like when it's honored. Walking the walk with your personal boundaries helps you establish your interpersonal parameters with solid footing.

Another way to incorporate this is to model the ways you appreciate boundary setting. Let's say that you reflected on some past boundaries and recognized that not being provided the opportunity to discuss and ask questions has historically left you confused and helpless. When possible, offering your recipient space to process and clarify can make the boundary more effective.

You can also offer kindness; give your recipient a chance to be seen. Let's say you're setting a boundary with someone who doesn't care for digital communication. Even if you'd prefer it, your boundary would likely be better received if you choose a more traditional form in which to convey it.

You can model how you wish to have boundaries set with you when you set boundaries with others. For example, prior to setting a boundary you could inquire with the other person to see if it's a good time for them to give you their attention. Making space for all parties demonstrates how boundaries can be set collaboratively. The good will and energy you offer in this instance will likely benefit you in both the immediate and the long term.

SEEK SUPPORT

Humility is paramount throughout the boundary-design journey. With every valuable step toward balance there will still be room for growth. But we don't have to be helpless in the face of this reality—we can instead seek support to help fill the void and facilitate the process. Approach those you trust requesting encouragement for the process, compassion for your challenges, feedback about your design, contrasting perspectives, and comparable experiences with boundaries. Seek additional knowledge: do research, listen to podcasts, check out workshops and classes. Consider soliciting aid from professional helpers such as therapists, consultants, or attorneys, who could appropriately address any significant underlying concerns. Individual, family, or group counseling, and support groups can help you as well as those you hope to set boundaries with.

CHAPTER 12

HEALING BOUNDARIES

Healing commences at the beginning of the boundary journey and persists throughout the process. Self-love engages us in attuning to our needs. This enhances our ability to proactively heal. Rather than leaving us stunned by catastrophe, self-love assists us in seeing opportunities to infuse healing before trouble spots erupt into bigger concerns.

Choosing to set boundaries grounded in self-love *is* healing in and of itself. Constantly committing to establishing healthy-boundary designs allows for continued catharsis. As you venture forward, new opportunities for healing may surface along your path, such as challenges to understand who you are and what you believe in. These may include how you find balance in the designing phase, or how to determine the level of firmness, what you want to disclose, and how you wish to share in the setting phase.

As a natural result of the deep dives required as part of the self-exploration throughout the boundary-design process, old wounds may surface. This could include old wounds you believed you'd tended to and fully healed, such as past unhealthy experiences with boundaries, as well as old wounds that are entirely new to you, such as recognizing underlying generational trauma, familial patterns, or unjust social systems. You could also become bruised along the way, perhaps from a challenging context, a toxic dynamic, or even your own inner bully. Forming the habit of processing throughout your boundary design journey, especially when you encounter these lesions, permits you to connect to insight about what may be curative for you.

While healing is possible and encouraged in creation and assertion, it is the primary focus in the third phase of the boundary-design process. Therefore, this chapter emphasizes the continued healing that persists following the establishment of a boundary. It includes self-soothing after a boundary is received, reupholstering your parameter when revisiting your boundary, and recovering when boundaries have been bashed.

BOUNDARY RECEPTION

The first segment of the healing phase is reception. This includes how you respond to your own boundaries. When it comes to core boundaries, you may have underlying uncertainty that makes you hesitate in response to your boundary—even though it was your decision to create it. For example, someone with a gluten allergy may wish to form a boundary around diet but worry that it's impossible. When it comes to peripheral boundaries, especially those set in haste, you may lack confidence in your methods, which can also reduce your reception to your own parameter. This can happen when, for example, an individual has decided to end a relationship but worries about how the other person will react.

Reception also includes how others respond to your boundaries. This may range from warm to frigid, and can occur the moment you convey your boundary or long after. Fortunately, healing is possible regardless of the reception. This healing begins with your response to how your boundary is received.

REFLECTION

To better understand boundary reception, consider the times that you have been on the receiving end of a boundary. How did you respond? How do you believe your response affected the dynamic?

_____

_____

_____

_____

_____

_____

INITIAL RECEPTION

As you might imagine, people's responses to boundaries usually occur right when they're communicated. The response may be welcoming, which we'll refer to here as a "warm" reception. The response may be unclear, which we'll refer to here as a "tepid" reception. Or the response may be resisted, which we'll refer to here as a "cold" reception. Recognizing the temperature of the response can help inform your healing, and choosing the response of healing can ultimately strengthen your boundary design.

WARM RECEPTION

As we explored earlier, a common misconception is that people often see boundaries as being a system of defense (see page 26). While this is often true, there are exceptions. In reality, healthy boundaries are about not just what is repelled but also what is fostered. If you find boundary design challenging, it may be hard to imagine that others won't bristle at your boundary. However, I encourage you to keep your mind and heart open to the possibility that your boundary can be received well.

You're able to receive your own core boundaries warmly when you are intentional in the boundary-design process. Even if they're challenging to form, their reception can be founded in your gratitude for your willingness to create necessary boundaries and your admiration for your commitment to the process. You may also receive your own boundary well if you experience a sense of alignment. You may feel at peace with your newfound integration and begin to reap the benefits you hoped would be possible from designing a healthy boundary.

A warm reception from others may encompass comfort of communication, kindness, appreciation, and respect. Recipients may be genuinely interested and invested in learning about your boundary in order to better adhere to it. Some may share their appreciation and thank you for your disclosure. Others may express compassion for the courage it required for you to share with them. If applicable, some may also express an apology. When a boundary is received warmly, allow yourself to consider the following questions: What may have helped your boundary be received warmly? What differs in this case compared to others? What can you incorporate from this experience for future boundaries? If you find yourself surprised at your welcomed boundary, reflect on the reality that a warm reception is possible.

TEPID RECEPTION

You may receive an indifferent response to your boundary. Oftentimes the individual is simply processing the new information. Other times their hesitance may be about what your boundary will mean for them. Sometimes they simply have mixed emotions about the boundary.

Try to remember that, though the boundary is important to you, it's not necessarily top priority to someone else. This doesn't necessarily mean that they don't respect you or your parameters; it could simply be a result of their current circumstances. The same person might have responded warmly to your boundary if they hadn't been overwhelmed at the time. It's helpful, when possible, to first inquire if the recipient has the bandwidth for you to share something that's important to you. Doing so can cultivate reciprocity and respect, which can improve the chances for a warm response when you finally divulge your message.

Sometimes you immediately know the response is tepid. Other times you may see signs such as visible reluctance or conflicting words and actions. Ideally you can respond in the moment, because a tepid response left unattended can devolve into a cold response. To avoid that, you can express your commitment to the relationship, ask questions, practice patience, offer collaboration, and make intentional changes. A tepid response has the potential to be healing for all involved.

COLD RECEPTION

Some boundaries immediately get an icy response. As explored earlier in chapter 3, there are a variety of reasons in which someone may respond poorly to your boundary (see "Common Reasons Why Boundaries Are Hard to Receive" on page 37). A few include selfishness, projection, and fears of neglect and abandonment. Some cold reactions include interrogations, passive-aggressive remarks, direct conflict, and explicit refusal to respect your boundary. Of course, none of us wants to experience this sort of response. Fortunately, we can respond just as we would for a tepid response—though it may require more effort and energy. In addition, self-care and self-love at large may be called for to heal the wounds of one's boundary being poorly received. Further, in some instances resources for the recipient can help both parties to heal from what underlies the frigid response. For example, when setting boundaries with someone who is struggling with alcoholism, seeking therapy, pursuing sobriety, and/or attending a support group can foster growth. In some instances, collaborative healing is possible by having a courageous conversation, seeking mediation, learning together, and/or starting joint counseling.

DELAYED REACTIONS

The healthy-design process is neither rigid or linear. It makes space for the reality that not all reactions to your boundaries will be immediate. Plus, as contexts, people, and considerations change, responses to boundaries may alter as well. Reactions may warm, especially if healing persists. However, responses may also cool over time. Acknowledging this change can help you to widen your perspective to healing. Even in the situations when defensiveness develops, healing is always possible as long as you continue tending to it. As time passes, checking in with the recipient can help you learn what maintenance is warranted so you can invest in healing.

BOUNDARY INFRACTIONS

Of course, times when a boundary gets pushback are some of the most difficult moments of the boundary journey. These transgressions can occur for a variety of reasons, from varying intentions. Some infractions occur unintentionally, such as when someone misunderstands the boundary, or genuinely forgets. Unfortunately, sometimes people intentionally violate boundaries, even recklessly or violently. Boundary transgressions are particularly common when a boundary is new, since old habits die hard, and new habits take time to form. But infractions can occur at any time.

Some oversteps are more challenging than others. The level of potency is usually a formula of several factors, all measured by your subjectivity. Some infractions may feel like gentle nudges, whereas others may feel like fully-fledged attacks. Knowing what likely lies behind a strong violation can help to inform your boundary-design process.

✏️ SPECTRUM OF BOUNDARY INFRACTION

Take a moment to think about times when you experienced boundary infractions. In the space following, write a brief sentence describing each infraction.

1. _____

2. _____

3. _____

4. _____

5. _____

6. _____

7. _____

8. _____

9. _____

10. _____

Next, on the numbered line below, add a keyword from each example at the number that best represents the intensity of the infraction—with "0" being "zero distress" and "10" being "violent distress."

• • • • • • •

What do you notice about the examples on the lower end of the spectrum? What do you notice about the examples on the higher end of the spectrum? How may your boundary design differ for a slight infraction versus a strong infraction?

THE NEED TO REVISIT BOUNDARIES

When we're in a vulnerable state, we may have a heightened response to boundary infractions and can be more likely to perceive infractions as strong violations. On the other hand, when we have well-designed boundaries and are in equilibrium, while we won't be immune to the pressure of an infraction, we're less likely to be thrown off-kilter by it. Nevertheless, since boundaries are protective measures, it's normal for us to feel defensive when our boundaries are infringed upon. Knowing what is more likely to trigger us can help in boundary design, as it can help identify where stronger boundaries are warranted. To follow are examples of reasons you may react strongly to boundary infractions.

THE BOUNDARY IS IMPORTANT TO YOU

The most obvious reason that a boundary infraction may pack more power is if the boundary is very important to you. While all boundaries you invest in will matter to some degree, some will likely matter more than others. Boundaries are built to guard what is most purposeful to us, such as who we are and what we believe. Therefore, if a boundary is designed to protect a very important aspect of ourselves, we may be more likely to safeguard that parameter and can be more dedicated to that boundary overall. Since interpersonal boundaries are essentially layers of our personal parameters, all boundaries are personal to some degree. However, those that are closer to your heart may be more hurtful when challenged. For example, let's say someone with a laid-back personality deeply values their family. While they may rarely be confrontational, if someone hurts a loved one they may enforce their boundary more stringently.

IT'S WIDELY ACKNOWLEDGED

While boundaries can vary from person to person and context to context, some do apply broadly. When a boundary is widely acknowledged, there's a general assumption that it doesn't need to be explicitly outlined. For a minor example, if you get your driver's license and offer to drive someone somewhere, you assume they won't quiz you on the difference between a red and green light. But a societal boundary being broken can hit harder; it's not simply a misunderstanding against one person—it's a violation of a commonly accepted norm.

The boundaries that seem to be universal often imbue the basis of humanity. For example, the belief that violence is wrong tends to be globally acknowledged. So when someone is violent with another, the violation of the recipient's basic human rights may cause more pain than the physical damage.

YOU HAVE A HISTORY WITH THE BOUNDARY

The sturdiness of a boundary, and the corresponding perceived intensity of the infraction, is heavily dependent on the boundary's creator. Oftentimes we don't have the luxury of setting boundaries with all people at once. The cycle of creating, asserting, and healing can vary for different relationships and contexts. If you have a boundary that you've recently invested in, that may be a more vulnerable space for you. Additionally, due to the newness of the boundary, it is likely that you will encounter a set of encroachments, especially at the onset, but also as the boundary settles into place in your world.

Let's say you have a boundary that's very important to you that people have trouble respecting. Note that, since it can take time for people to adjust to and honor a boundary, they're not necessarily intending to be disrespectful. If Gerard is worn thin by the energy required to maintain his boundary, even a small infraction could make a huge impact. Or, for another example, let's say you sprain your ankle playing basketball. You heal over time. Years later, you sprain it again while running. It's not the particular sport that's the trigger; the sheer existence of the injury creates the susceptibility, even after healing.

With a cumulative consideration, a large number of small infractions over time have aggregated to have a large effect. On top of this, if it's a boundary that you personally struggle to respect, it can be triggering to have someone else infract it, since that lays bare the difficulty of your struggle. Using the example of the ankle sprained playing basketball, if you stubbornly push through the healing process in order to play in the next game, you're more likely to get reinjured. What's more, a repeat injury could worsen the original concern, and you may find yourself even more frustrated.

THE POWER OF THE PUSHER

Beyond having a history with the boundary itself, if you have a history with the person pushing your boundary that could intensify the experience. Let's say you've had multiple conversations with someone about your boundary; each time you have to reiterate your parameters, you're likely to grow in frustration. For example, let's say longtime friends Manuel and Prem decide to share an apartment. Several months in, Manuel is a few days late on his rent. A few months later, he is a week late, and then again the next month. Each time, Prem covers him to avoid issues with their building management. And each time, Prem shares his concerns, and Manuel promises to be prompt in the future. Then one day, Prem grabs milk from the fridge to find there's only three sips left in the carton. He blows up at Manuel about how irresponsible he is. This example illustrates the fact that multiple boundaries can exist between any two people. In this case, though Manuel leaving just three sips in the milk carton is technically a small infraction, it compounds with the ongoing disrespect that Prem feels about how Manuel handles his financial obligations.

Simply having history with someone, even if they don't have a record of pushing your boundaries, can affect the intensity of an infraction. This is often the case if the person is close to you. While it might not be a fair assumption, we often like to think that our loved ones know us well. This encompasses what matters to us, and where our boundaries can be found. Hence, we might feel more offended if a person close to us breaks a boundary than if a stranger does. Instead of taking the infraction at face value, we may perceive it as an offense to the relationship itself.

Sometimes the person with the most power to harm your boundaries is yourself. When you don't abide by your own boundaries, this self-sabotage doesn't just hinder your personal parameters; it reduces the efficacy of your interpersonal boundaries as well. If you're not accountable to your own boundaries, you cannot ethically hold others to a higher standard than you're willing to demonstrate for yourself.

People tend to overfocus on interpersonal parameters, but doing so can make us feel disempowered. If you want to have a boundary of respectful communication, does that mean that self-deprecating humor is unacceptable? It's important to emphasize that, if others see that you poorly maintain a personal parameter, there's a risk that they will also infringe on your boundary. This reality is often a tough pill to swallow; it can be difficult to sit with the truth that you may have hindered your own boundary effectiveness.

📁 SAVI

Let's revisit Savi's experience at yoga class, when the new instructor announced the class would include adjustments unless anyone objected. To recollect what we know about Savi, see pages 36, 153, and 155.

First, what boundary transgression(s) do you notice in this scenario?

_____

_____

_____

_____

Using what you've learned about Savi, what would you do if you were in her shoes?

_____

_____

_____

_____

Depending on where she is in her healing journey, she may find it empowering to advocate for herself in that moment. She also could just be triggered. Although she doesn't feel comfortable with a stranger touching her body, she'd also feel uncomfortable being the ostracized outsider. Of course, there is no right or wrong choice of what she does next, as long as it serves her.

BREACHED BOUNDARIES

Earlier you learned that attuning your self-awareness can help you to attempt to prevent, and hopefully reduce, the amount of challenges you encounter in your boundary-design process (see page 47). Breaching is a common difficulty people experience in cultivating healthy boundaries. The simple truth is, it's not a matter of *if* one of your boundaries will ever be crossed; it's a matter of *when*. And though some of us often jump to conclusions, the fact is that a boundary infraction doesn't necessarily mean that a boundary was poorly designed, that the crosser had malicious intent, that aggressive defense is warranted, or that we're incapable of having healthy boundaries. Despite our best efforts, over time a crossing of some kind, however severe, is inevitable. We can accept this fact without needing to also accept the infractions when they occur.

Redefining your perspective of boundaries can help you to prepare for boundary crossings. This enhanced perspective can strengthen your boundaries, and ultimately yourself, since it helps you to tend to them effectively. When you acknowledge the degree of the infraction and respond with the energy appropriate to tend to that wound, healing is possible. Healing is a self-loving choice in which we seek to gather the inertia of a setback and use it to cultivate growth. At this juncture, you can celebrate your progress, even if it is simply a learned lesson, and courageously choose to mend as you continue on your path.

FINDING THE LINE

In order to appropriately discern when a boundary has been breached, you must qualify what counts as an infraction. Where is the line between what is permitted and what is discouraged? To help elucidate where the line is, it can be beneficial to reflect on what lies on both sides. Generally speaking, you'd likely consider someone barging through your door as a breach. What *would* be permitted in this situation? What if the person knocked at your door? Begin with a broad consideration and then explore relevant specifics. In the given scenario, there's a huge difference between if the person is the mail carrier versus if the person had been specifically asked to stay away. What if we take this a step further and factor in a restraining order: just the person being at the door, knocking or not, would be unacceptable. On the other hand, what if the person coming through the door lives with you? We wouldn't expect them to knock at their own front door. But if we take it a step further and clarify whether we're discussing the front door versus, say, a bedroom door or bathroom door, the line may shift as well.

REFLECTION

How do you define a boundary infraction?

_____

_____

_____

_____

SIGNS YOUR BOUNDARY IS BEING PUSHED

Once you're able to distinguish where the line is located, you're able to heighten your awareness to the signs that your boundary is being pushed. When a boundary is breached, there may be changes in your thoughts, emotions, and behaviors. Sometimes signs are subtle, such as a twinge of irritation. Some are so subtle they can surface without our realizing they're tethered to a violation. On the other hand, for some an aggressive boundary push can feel like a punch in the gut.

An infringement can have an effect on you even before you realize it's happening. So it's ideal to learn how to quickly recognize an overstep, since keen attunement to these signs can assist in timely recovery. At minimum, when you recognize an infraction you can swiftly tend to self-care in order to better regain equilibrium. In addition, you might consider if boundary editing is applicable. For example, recognizing a boundary has been breached may indicate that your boundary could be better delineated. Finally, you can choose how to respond to the infraction itself—which might range from taking time for self-reflection to employing strategies of self-defense.

With continued investment in healthy boundary design, you'll familiarize yourself with signs that your boundary is being pushed, by yourself or by someone else. You'll be able to use the warning signs to proactively tend to your parameters. In addition, lessons can be synthesized over time. As a part of that healing process, allow yourself space to retroactively consider signs that a boundary was infringed upon. Doing so can help you to heighten your awareness and potentially better attune in the future.

REFLECTION

What are signs that someone is pushing on your boundary? What would you notice in yourself? What would you notice in someone else?

✎ THE DEGREE OF THE INFRACTION

In addition to knowing *where* a boundary line exists, it's also helpful to assess the degree of the infraction. Just as boundaries vary, intensity tends to differ from breach to breach as well. Returning to the door examples in the Finding the Line section earlier, there's a large difference between a roommate barging into a room and a violent stranger barging in.

Explore the diverse words used to describe varied levels of infractions and place them on the lines below, with "0" being lowest and "10" being highest. For example, a slight boundary breach may be called a *nudge, push,* or *overstep,* whereas an aggressive breach may be called an *insult, offense, blow,* or *violation.*

1. _____   6. _____

2. _____   7. _____

3. _____   8. _____

4. _____   9. _____

5. _____   10. _____

Revisit your core and peripheral boundaries (see the activities in chapter 9). Choose at least five examples and place them where they fit along the spectrum. You may find it helpful to review the reflection regarding the firmness of your boundaries (see page 150), since the intensity of an infraction tends to parallel the firmness of a boundary.

For each boundary, consider what it looks like when it's encroached. How would you know if the boundary is being pushed? What are the signs you'd observe from yourself and/or others?

· · · · · · ·

ADDRESSING BOUNDARY INFRACTIONS

Tending to a breached boundary requires the balance of promptly handling the infraction while offering yourself ample time to recover and reintegrate. When your boundary is crossed, you're likely to be pushed off-kilter. To effectively heal, you must attempt to regain equilibrium. Hence, with each breach—at minimum—an acknowledgment and subsequent self-care are warranted for healing. Beyond self-care, the ingredients in your remedy will vary based on the degree of the infraction. While one breach may call for a simple acknowledgment to yourself, a more intense breach could call for clarifying your boundary and perhaps increasing the consequences. Even stronger infractions may call for editing your boundary altogether.

✎ ASSESSING BOUNDARY INFRACTIONS

Revisit the case examples and the boundary infractions that each person experiences. Put yourself in each person's shoes. Based on your core boundaries, how would you assess the intensity of each breach they experience? Place their names on the line below, with 1 being mildly intense to 10 being very intense.

| 0 | 1 | 2 | 3 | 4 | 5 | 6 | 7 | 8 | 9 | 10 |

Person	What was the breach?	How would you address the infraction?
Parker		
Corinne		
Dave		
Rae		
Maria		

Person	What was the breach?	How would you address the infraction?
Savi		

· · · · · · ·

BOUNDARY BUFFERS

Tending to a boundary over time is crucial in the healthy boundary-design process. When it comes to breached boundaries, being cognizant of oversteps and your tolerance of them offers helpful data to integrate into your journey. Some boundaries may warrant your conveying something that is clear, concise, and concrete. These are the boundaries for vulnerable areas for which a breach would be entirely unacceptable, and potentially even aggressive. For example, if you believe there are no situations when physical violence would be permissible, then you know you will never tolerate direct harm.

Some boundaries don't require the same rigidity. This is especially common with newer or softer boundaries, as well as collaborative boundaries. While of course you'd still prefer to have your boundary honored, in these instances you may also be able to infuse grace, humility, and patience into the situation. Change, habits, and boundaries require time. Adopting an absolute approach to your boundary threshold can cause you to develop an unnecessarily defensive stance. In healthy boundary design, responding to a breach with a cooperative, collaborative mindset can help ensure your boundary is understood in practice as well as in theory.

For firmer boundaries, you may not have the ability to tolerate oversteps. But for less firm boundaries, you may be able to offer the space for unintentional pushes to be clarified, discussed, and collaborated upon. Regardless of where a boundary lies across the spectrum, it's beneficial to consider your threshold for all your parameters.

For which boundaries will you not permit a push of any kind? How many oversteps are you willing to withstand for each parameter? Which boundaries would benefit from a buffer for oversteps?

The healing phase isn't just for tending to individual boundary breaches; it also encompasses a wider understanding of your boundaries, including their efficacy. Allowing yourself space to zoom out and take in this broader perspective can assist in aggregating boundary data and highlighting where maintenance is warranted.

REVISITING

Revisiting your boundaries helps to keep them maintained and effective. Consider it like an oil change for your vehicle: a standard, important task that ensures everything is functioning smoothly. It's maintenance that's too important to neglect.

Given that fact, try to create a habit of returning to your previously established parameters to check in. Proactively tending to your boundaries can help to promptly address concerns and potentially evade grave problems. You may find that a routine of revisiting works best for you. Perhaps use your birthday as a reminder to tend to this essential piece of your self-care. But that's for routine check-ins. You'll also want to revisit your boundaries when you encounter chapter changes in your life, such as beginning a relationship, ending a relationship, leaving your job, or starting a new one. Then, of course, you'll want to revisit boundaries when you experience a breach of some kind.

Regardless of why you revisit your boundaries, healing is always possible. It's an opportunity to reevaluate your previous creation and incorporate new information to enhance your parameters. The process of revisitation begins by returning to your base, the established safe zone to help you recalibrate as you encounter challenges in your path (see the Returning to Your Base activity on page 140). From there, you can prioritize checking in with both your core boundaries (see page 144) and your peripheral boundaries (see page 147). Reconsidering what you wish to cultivate, protect, release, and repel across these layers can inform how your current boundaries warrant amending. The supplemental reflections that assisted in initially forming your parameters can help you develop a keener perspective of your present boundary needs. Applying a SWOT assessment (see page 155), and analyzing it against your completed chart in the Connecting to Your Core activity (see page 141), can empower you with the details you need to recover.

SCAFFOLDING

When you take a moment to reevaluate your boundaries, you may notice gaps that hinder your boundary design. For example, being unclear about your core boundaries could add confusion to your peripheral boundaries. On the other hand, sometimes our experiences shed light on a gap we'd previously overlooked, such as experiencing something that feels like a breach but that you'd not anticipated being problematic. Whether or not these openings warrant interpersonal attention, they always require intrapersonal attention. Fortunately, you can fortify your boundaries with clarifications and modifications through the process of scaffolding.

CLARIFICATIONS

When revisiting your boundaries, you may recognize that some details are unclear and warrant improvement. Perhaps you've gained insight and can clarify details that were already unclear to you. Or perhaps you've realized that details you found clear weren't as clear to others. Or, following a boundary infraction, you may recognize that reiterating your parameters can help to prevent a similar breach in the future. Adding clarity can aid all these scenarios.

MODIFICATIONS

When revisiting your boundaries, you might find that changes are required as well. Oftentimes a mere tweak to your old boundary will suffice. More influential occurrences—such as a substantial growth curve, an eventful moment, or a significant infraction—can warrant a range of changes.

Additional modifications could involve shifts in how you approach the boundary at large, such as the self-love you infuse in the boundary or the options of practicing acceptance, letting go, or walking away.

EMERGENCIES

Of course, emergencies will thrust you into the revisiting phase (see "Is It Worth It?" on page 34). In times of hardship, though it can feel overwhelming to maintain your boundaries, you might find that returning to your core and reexperiencing that tether can help you to find your footing as you resiliently continue forward. Your core connection permits you to fortify as needed in order to weather the storm as best you can. In some moments, it may even cue you to release your reins. Then, when the sky clears again, you might return to your previous parameters as they were, or you may find that healing is needed. In some cases, healing might amount to revisiting the emergency boundaries you put up in the chaos of the storm, or patching a fault that the emergency laid bare.

PERSISTENT PUSHER

We've already noted that people will sometimes push on your boundaries; this is to be expected. But what if this becomes a pattern? Unfortunately, there are people who will repeatedly push your buttons. I call this type of person a "professional pusher." They may push on one of your boundaries often, push multiple boundaries, push multiple boundaries often, push multiple people's boundaries, push multiple boundaries of multiple people, or even push multiple boundaries of multiple people multiple times! Sometimes people like this don't comprehend the importance of having personal codes. So, if they can't adhere to their own ideal boundaries, they certainly can't honor anyone else's. Also, you might find that clarifications and modifications aren't always effective with a persistent pusher. However, healing is still possible.

In some situations, it can be beneficial to consider what prompts the person to repeatedly overstep boundaries, since doing so can help you heighten your awareness, tailor your strategies, and potentially offer compassion. Sometimes a persistent pusher is living with a condition that inhibits their ability to respect other's boundaries—perhaps a mental health diagnosis, or insufficiently coping with a physical diagnosis. Perhaps they lack cognitive development, like a crawling baby who can't comprehend what objects or surfaces are unsafe. Many such boundary breaches are unintentional. With a few edits in our expectations, explanations, and parameters, we can do much to bridge the gap between our boundaries and those who interact with them. Of course, it can't be denied that some persistent pushers are intentional—perhaps also careless, reckless, and even dangerous. Boundaries serve their ultimate purpose with this form of pusher. In this kind of situation, the healing that's called for is to continue to invest in your self-love as you persevere in your boundary commitment, despite others' violent tendencies. Sometimes healing in this scenario may encompass your ability to accept reality, forgive yourself, step back, and let go.

RECOVERING

With adequate investment, many boundaries can be maintained and even improved over time. Unfortunately, this is not always the case. With some boundaries, it's important to consider the line at which continued investment would negatively impact your well-being. In instances such as repeat breaches, severe infraction, or mere exhaustion, the step forward may be to just let go. While it is true that healing is possible throughout the boundary-design journey, sometimes it's not possible to include everyone in that healing. The priority in recovery is the self-love required to keep you on your broader journey despite any injuries you've encountered along the way. Loving yourself during this vulnerable period allows you to recognize your needs and pursue them with humility, patience, grace, and compassion. It enables you to manage what you are able to manage—and to ask for help with everything else.

REST

Rest is an integral component when recovering from boundary challenges. Indeed, sufficient rest is essential throughout your journey, such as when you take a moment to pause and step back, or even to move away from a challenge. In this therapeutic space you can recharge by tending to your core. Once you've recalibrated your personal boundaries, you're better able to reflect, integrate information, broaden your perspectives, practice patience, and strategize for the future.

FORGIVENESS

Sometimes being aware of the challenges in the boundary-design process opens your eyes to the reality that there's something you need to let go of, and sometimes that letting go calls for forgiveness. Forgiveness is possible when we combine the humble acknowledgment of what occurred, accountability of what occurred, and genuine compassion for its effect from a mindset that denounces perfection, supports growth, and fosters healing.

Note that forgiveness is not to be confused with excusing, condoning, minimizing, or ignoring. Forgiveness is simply an essential step in permitting yourself to let go of a past occurrence. Even when intentions are pure, mishaps will happen from time to time. In these moments, you may have the opportunity to grow through forgiveness.

Consider the experiences you've had with forgiveness. Have there been times when forgiveness came easily? If so, what do you think made that possible? Have there been times when forgiveness was challenging? If so, do you know why that was?

OFFERING FORGIVENESS

Offering forgiveness in the boundary process can help you to untangle yourself from strings that tie you to the past. Without releasing these tethers, you can become stuck in old patterns that impede healthy boundaries—and, subsequently, your personal and interpersonal wellness. But note that offering forgiveness doesn't necessarily mean that you condone what occurred. Similarly, for interpersonal boundaries, forgiveness doesn't necessarily equate with reconciliation. Also, while receiving an apology can be gratifying, and can even serve as a catalyst for mutual healing, it is unreliable to expect an apology will follow your expression of forgiveness. This is because if you require an apology in order to move forward, you give the other person power in your life. Further, being roped to this requisite can weigh you down and impede your boundaries and ultimately your wellness.

Forgiveness is offered in the boundary-design process when you wish to let go of aspects of past boundaries that may be weighing down the effectiveness of present boundaries. In general, it's easier to forgive a mild, single boundary breach than a stronger, recurrent violation. Unfortunately, the conundrum is that it's the stronger, recurrent violations that tend to keep us chained. As it happens, it's in just this sort of scenario that you can benefit from forgiving someone for something they are unable to apologize for.

REFLECTION

Think about your boundary-design process to date. In what ways can you grow by forgiveness?

_____

_____

_____

_____

SEEKING FORGIVENESS

In order to seek forgiveness you must recognize wrongdoing, take responsibility for the part you played, and commit yourself to the learned lesson(s) at hand. When you embark on this challenging path, you risk falling into spirals of embarrassment, sadness, shame, guilt, and anxiety. This may include things that you regret saying, doing, ignoring, or even neglecting. Without self-love, tripping into these areas can devolve into feelings of inferiority and inadequacy. In short, if you seek forgiveness from this unsteady foundation, it may not be (as) effective for you or the other person.

Self-love can both help prevent boundary slips and heal the injuries when they do occur. Even when we try our utmost best, misunderstandings occur. Since no one is perfect, seeking forgiveness can be a helpful practice in humbly recognizing an area for growth and pledging to improve that domain. Then, you're able to commit to healing yourself in order to effectively seek forgiveness from others. Note, too, that when you humbly seek genuine forgiveness, offering an apology helps you to express empathy, take responsibility, and assert your intentions for the future.

REFLECTION

Think about your boundary-design process to date. In what ways can you grow by seeking forgiveness?

_____

_____

_____

_____

SELF-FORGIVENESS

When we think about forgiveness an interpersonal exchange often comes to mind. Yet, many times the person you need to seek forgiveness from is yourself. Further, effective forgiveness begins with yourself. This form of forgiveness is often overlooked—and, unfortunately, avoiding self-forgiveness comes with consequences. The inability to forgive yourself has been associated with anxiety, depression, and a weakened immune system. On the other hand, choosing to forgive yourself can decrease the negative effects of guilt, demonstrate your respect for yourself, and allow you to foster your growth.

You must first practice grace, patience, and compassion with yourself before being able to genuinely offer these to others. As a self-loving act, self-forgiveness allows you to learn from your previous experiences, accept responsibility, take accountability, and set your intentions to learn and grow in the future. Note, though, that since you are both the forgiver and the one being forgiven, self-forgiveness can be a difficult process.

The struggle to forgive is a common obstacle in designing healthy boundaries. Exacerbating the struggle is the fact that the pain resulting from the lack of accessible healing impedes the ability to offer forgiveness. In these moments, the momentum of boundary progress must be paused. Experiencing guilt for something you have done, such as encroaching on someone's boundary, can keep you stuck in time. The sentiment of shame can quickly spiral into feelings of inferiority and inadequacy, greatly hindering your ability to design healthy boundaries. Similarly, when someone has encroached on your boundary, progress can be stalled by feelings of sadness, disappointment, confusion, frustration, anger, resentment, or rage. Therefore, in such moments your opportunity to grow comes from offering yourself the love you need to allow space for these emotions to run their course—prior to embarking on the next phase of healing: self-forgiveness.

REFLECTION

Think about your boundary-design process to date. In what ways can you grow by forgiving your-self?

ACCEPTANCE

A nuanced form of forgiveness is acceptance. Acceptance can be achieved with an apology and collaboration, but neither is required. Sometimes in the boundary-design process there comes a time when you realize you've reached the limit of what you're willing to invest. Most often this occurs in relation to interpersonal boundaries. When you arrive at an impasse, you can humbly offer yourself acceptance you are better able to acknowledge and allow space for the imperfection of others. Self-love equips you with the ability to offer compassion for others' struggles. Take for example an instance when someone you care about pushes on your boundary. While this is traditionally seen as an offense, the healthy-design process allows for the consideration that not all such instances are done with harmful intent. Your loved ones may be working hard to improve their confidence, challenge unhealthy thoughts, break toxic patterns, and offer both themselves and you respect. In these moments, your kindness can offer a collaboration that may pave the path for an improved boundary design. Whether or not others seek grace, you may be able to offer yourself a safe buffer by knowing when you need to step back, or even remove yourself altogether. Should you ever come to think that any further investment—be that a clarification, exception, or apology—would do more harm than good, you may wish to relinquish your tether altogether. You do not need to pour continued commitment into a process that is harming you.

Should you find yourself at such a juncture, you have an opportunity to grow in self-acceptance. Practicing self-acceptance is loving yourself enough to choose to take a step away. Regarding boundary design, in such a moment you can recognize how far you've come and honor all your hard work—while also honoring that continued effort is not worth your while. This in and of itself becomes a boundary. It is a unique balance in which you can find happiness in your past efforts and contentment in your choice to let go.

REFLECTION

Think about your boundary-design process to date. Where do you have opportunities to grow in regard to self-acceptance?

Think about your boundary-design process to date. Where do you have opportunities to grow in acceptance beyond yourself?

_____

_____

_____

_____

_____

_____

LETTING GO

No one wants to be bogged down by toxic aspects of the past. Letting go is integral to the boundary-design process, as it allows for the levity and endurance required to press on. However, the act of releasing our unhelpful thoughts, unpleasant emotions, unhealthy patterns, and unwanted experiences calls for more effort than just the best of intentions.

Forgiveness and acceptance can assist in the process of letting go. Similar to both, letting go does not entail condoning, supporting, ignoring, undermining, or reconciling with what occurred. The act of letting go does not give anyone power over you; instead, it shifts your internal dynamic toward alignment. When you accept what occurred as is and hone forgiveness where possible, you are able to release what no longer serves you. Letting go allows for a sense of closure. With this calming effect, you are better able to find equilibrium in your journey. The energy that had previously been entangled becomes available for you to invest in other domains, such as with others who respect your boundaries, and in your own personal boundaries. In doing so, healthier boundaries are possible. (Note that the Healing Boundaries worksheet in the appendix aligns with the different sections in this chapter.)

REFLECTION

Where can you benefit from letting go?

_____

_____

_____

_____

_____

_____

_____

_____

_____

_____

_____

_____

_____

_____

_____

_____

_____

DESIGNING HEALTHY BOUNDARIES

CONCLUSION

Let's take a moment to pause. Place your hands on your heart. Offer yourself a deep inhale, and with your exhale release. As you continue to nurture yourself with this deep, intentional breath, scan for tension. If you find one, see if you can permit softness with each passing breath.

You've made it.

Whether this is your first cycle through this guide, or one of many, it is impossible to deny that this is hard work. Despite the challenge, here you are. The effort you have invested and continue to invest are an incredible act of self-love.

Albeit difficult, I hope that at this juncture in your journey you find yourself with a refreshed perspective, improved confidence, increased alignment, and strengthened connection to your core.

As you have witnessed, reflection is essential throughout the process of tailoring healthy boundaries. I hope that you utilize the worksheets in the appendix and revisit this guide as needed. I hope that you are energized to continue to create, set, and heal the boundaries you hold with yourself and others for the rest of your days to come.

Sending love and light for the path ahead,

Shainna

REFLECTION

How does your current view of boundaries compare to the view you held when you began this guide?

_____

_____

_____

_____

_____

_____

Review each self-love segment (see page 47) and use this diagram to assess your status. Take notes, rate from 1 to 10, or shade in your levels with different colors. Revisit this activity to better understand where you have strengths, where you have opportunities for growth, and how self-love can be infused into your healthy-design journey.

THE SEVEN SEGMENTS OF SELF-LOVE

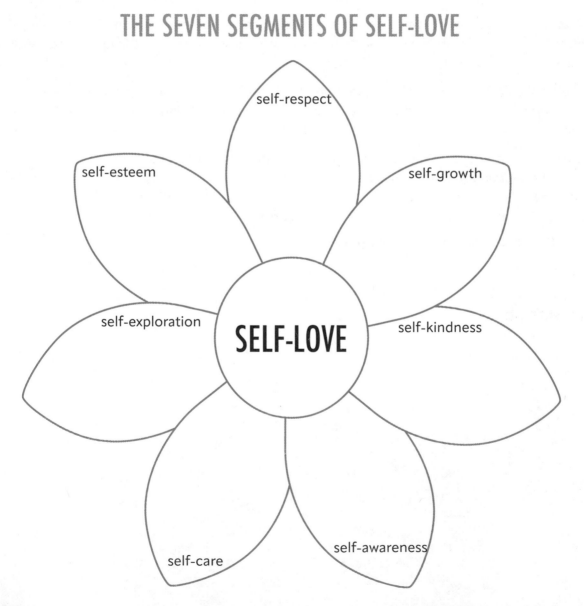

BOUNDARY DOMAINS

This worksheet can be used to connect to your domains as well as to your core boundaries. It can also be helpful when exploring initial domains and core boundaries. Additionally, completing this sheet over time can offer helpful data in tracking your boundary journey.

To follow are our four core questions. On the left side of each question, write numbered statements specifying something about this aspect of yourself that you wish to cultivate and protect. On the right side, write numbered statements specifying something about this aspect of yourself that you wish to release and repel. For example, if the question of "Who are you?" spurs someone to answer "an artist," then it may look like this:

Cultivate and Protect		Release and Repel
1. I wish to honor my originality. 2. I want to cultivate creativity. 3. I hope to protect my time to create.	**Who are you?** An artist	4. I want to let go of unconstructive criticism. 5. I want to release cruel inner judgment.
	What do you believe?	
	How do you find balance?	
	Where do you have the opportunity to grow?	

BOUNDARY LEVELS

This worksheet can be used to help you explore the levels in which your boundaries exist. Your personal boundaries exist at the core level. Use the additional layers to explore the dynamics that may exist in the peripheral layers. You may opt to put more than one category on the same level (e.g., family and friends). Use letters as you list your categories.

For example, we will all begin with **A** as personal boundaries. Building on the example for domains in chapter 9, potential peripheral layers may be:

Friends	**Employers**	**Neighbors**
Family	**Colleagues**	**Strangers**
Mentors	**Customers**	

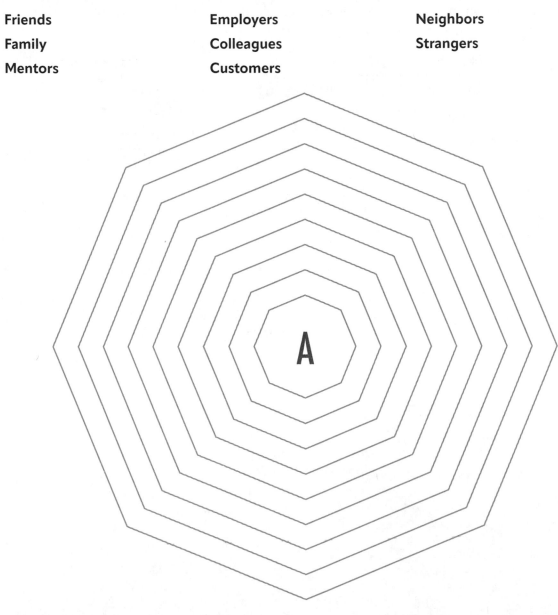

YOUR BOUNDARY CODE

This worksheet can assist you in better understanding your boundaries. This is intended to be used in conjunction with the boundary domains (page 189) and boundary levels (page 190) sheets just preceding this. When forming initial boundaries, begin by selecting one boundary domain at a time and commence with the core level. From there, you can build on each domain as you change levels. With each additional level, refer to your personal boundaries to promote boundary alignment. As you progress, you may notice that some boundaries may seem repetitive. This is a positive sign of your having consistency in your boundary code. This worksheet can also be helpful when you revisit boundaries in the healing phase.

Domain		Level
Technology	• Turn off all devices by 9 p.m. • Refrain from answering work emails after 5 p.m. • Prioritize spending device-free time weekly.	Personal

Domain		Level

MAPPING YOUR PERIPHERAL BOUNDARIES

Label the rings expanding beyond your core boundaries with the most common contexts you find yourself in (e.g., home, school, work, gym, stores, social events, and parks). Or, you could instead label the rings with your closest relationships (e.g., partner, family, friends, colleagues, acquaintances, neighbors, and strangers).

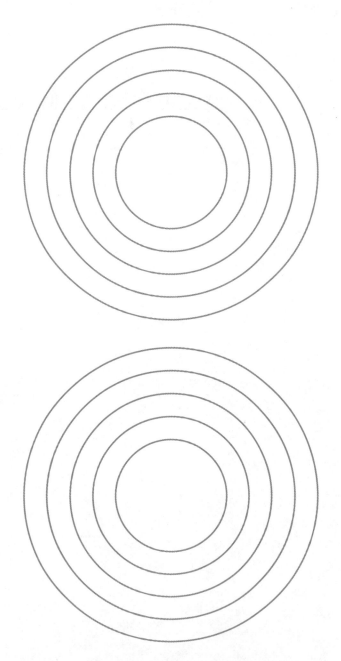

EXPLORING PERIPHERAL BOUNDARIES

Refer back to page 148 for a completed example of this worksheet.

Core boundary statement regarding the theme of: _____

_____

_____

_____

EXPLORING PERIPHERAL BOUNDARIES

Level	Boundary

EXPLORING PERIPHERAL BOUNDARIES

Level	Boundary

SETTING BOUNDARIES

This worksheet can be used to guide you in communicating a peripheral boundary as addressed on page 148. This chart can be used to explore key details for communicating a boundary. For each parameter, begin by revisiting your core—the "why" behind your boundary. Then, reflect on what it is you wish to set in place. Next, consider who needs to be informed and/or whom you wish to inform. Finally, consider how you wish to put your boundary in place.

Why is this boundary important?

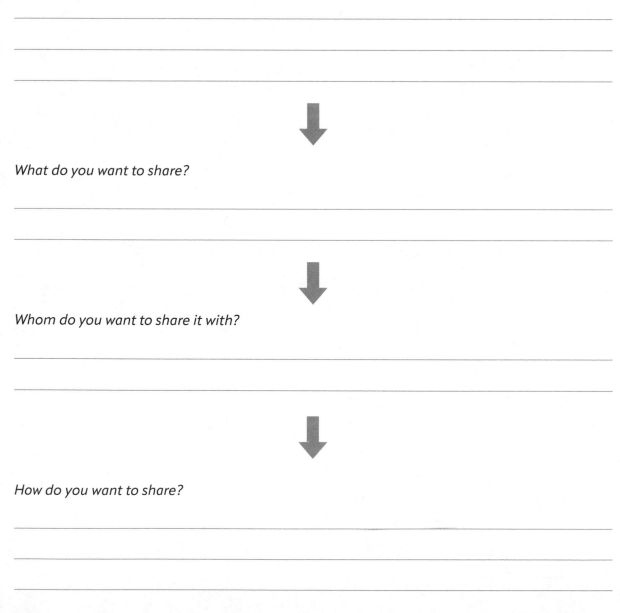

_____

_____

_____

What do you want to share?

_____

_____

Whom do you want to share it with?

_____

_____

How do you want to share?

_____

_____

_____

SWOT CHART

The SWOT chart can be used to deepen your boundary reflections by contemplating the strengths, weaknesses, opportunities, and threats in your present plan. For help completing this activity, see Setting Healthy Boundaries on page 149.

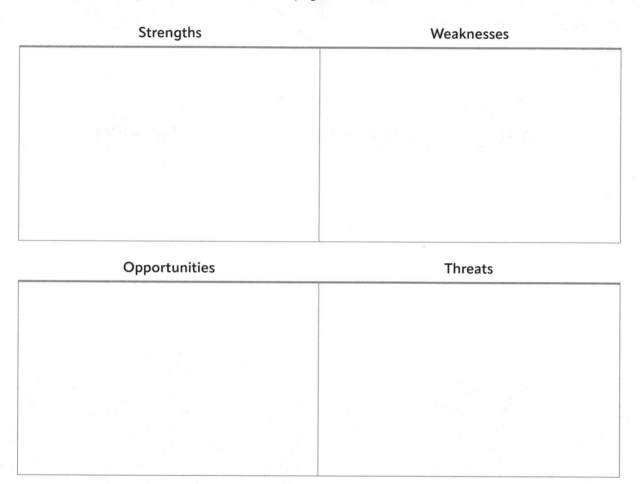

Strengths

Weaknesses

Opportunities

Threats

COMMUNICATING YOUR BOUNDARY

Consider a situation like Savi's on page 153, in which you need to communicate a boundary. Brainstorm some options for how to approach said boundary, then share your thoughts on the potential effects of each choice in the empty columns.

Situation: _____

_____

_____

Option	Potential Consequences	Potential Benefits

HEALING BOUNDARIES

This list of reflective questions can help you assess and improve your boundaries over time.

1. What is the boundary that warrants healing?

2. Did a boundary infraction occur? If not, skip to question 7.

3. What details do we know about the breach?

4. What is the intensity of the breach?

5. Who is involved in the breach?

6. Has this breach occurred previously? If yes, what measures were taken after?

7. What have you learned about this boundary?

8. Where are your opportunities for growth?

9. What of it can be managed? What is beyond your control?

10. How can you practice self-love to promote healing?

11. Is there an opportunity to scaffold your boundary?

12. Is there an opportunity to modify your boundary?

13. Is there an opportunity to practice forgiveness?

14. Is there an opportunity to practice acceptance?

15. Is there an opportunity to practice letting go?

16. How would you like to enhance this boundary?

ABOUT THE AUTHOR

Dr. Shainna Ali is a mental health counselor, educator, and advocate who is dedicated to highlighting the important role of mental health in fostering happiness, fulfillment, and overall wellness. She is the author of *The Self-Love Workbook*, *The Self-Love Workbook for Teens,* *The Self-Love Planner,* and *Luna Finds Love Everywhere*, and is the owner of Integrated Counseling Solutions, a counseling and consulting practice in Orlando, Florida. In her practice, she uses a strengths-based approach that empowers clients on their journey of self-love and mental wellness.

Within the field of mental health, her areas of expertise include exploring identity and culture, fostering emotional intelligence, healing from trauma, and utilizing creative counseling methods. When she isn't working, she invests in her self-love by practicing yoga, spending time with her loved ones, and exploring the world. To learn more, follow her on Instagram @DrShainna or visit www.DrShainna.com.